MW00627371

Critical Acclaim for *A Light in the Darkness*

People > anything else. This essential truth, often forgotten by organizations and leaders, is at the heart of this engaging and insightful book. Often hostage to a drive for short-term results, JC argues, we confuse building narrowly focused capabilities with the need for broader capacity that enables adaptation to changing conditions. This combat veteran's book is a must-read.
General Stanley McChrystal, U.S. Army, Retired
Co-founder and Partner, McChrystal Group

If there is one thing about JC that stands out, it is his character. The ideas in this book about Leadership, Teamwork and Selfless Service are concepts that are applicable to both the military and professional sports, which have many similarities, as well as to our everyday lives and jobs.
Ron Rivera
Head Coach, Carolina Panthers

Where so many authors have focused on leadership for effectiveness, what I love about this book is that it gives us not only a model for efficacy, but also a model for mastery in life. JC's focus on the need to think for oneself, take ownership, and prioritize direct experience over procedural knowledge makes this primer essential for everyone, especially women. As a woman and a global entrepreneur, I find that this book speaks directly to those of us who are trying to rewrite the manual and not merely follow it.

When Glick says that "having a leadership responsibility is to be responsible for developing and caring for people," he reorients what we value in our leaders and our understanding of gender roles. Our historical image of an authoritative, patriarchal figure who commands compliance melts away into a far more balanced image. Listening becomes more important than knowing.

Leili Gerami
Chairman, LEGE Investments

In the K-12 education sector, I often hear (and myself have used) the phrase, "We must prepare students to compete for jobs that don't exist." It is a compelling and appropriate goal for our schools and teachers. Such "preparation" in our schools, however, often translates into what JC Glick refers to as building "capabilities," doubling down on ensuring that students show proficiency in meeting standards.

While such proficiency is necessary, stopping there is selling our young people short and doesn't truly prepare them for the unknown. Preparing students for this unknown future requires a both-and approach to learning: it is both ensuring that our students are capable of demonstrating proficiency and providing them opportunities to cultivate capacity. This insightful book presents a framework that brings this both-and approach to life.

What does capacity-building look like in the classroom? It looks like students engaging in a design process with a diverse set of teammates, embracing failure as a growth opportunity, and adapting to circumstances that do not have clear solutions. In this environment, as psychologist Carol Dweck would say, when students are presented with a problem that's a bit too hard to solve, they respond not by believing they are not smart enough to solve it, but that they have just not solved it yet. Our education institutions must shift to this both capability and capacity approach to teaching, learning, and leading.

This book's message – gleaned from personal experience in the military and sharpened by examples from across sectors – is particularly essential for education policy and practice in the 21st century and beyond. This book's message is critical if we want to set our students up to compete for jobs that do not yet exist.
Ansel Sanders, Ed.L.D.
President and CEO, Public Education Partners

There've been a few situations in my life where I needed a coach or mentor. Without hesitation, I always called JC. His greatest ability is to help you see the situation objectively and align it with your personal vision in a way that enables moral and ethical clarity. Most impressively, you never feel like he's telling you how to solve the problem. You end up feeling like you figured it out yourself. That is real leadership. This book is going to help a lot of people.
Tony Blauer
CEO & Founder, Blauer Tactical Systems, Inc.

JC Glick stumbles upon some of the hardest and most daunting questions in human learning: Are we teaching in the best way possible? How can we create better ways of teaching in the complex environment of the globalized world? What skills will be fundamental now and in the future to addressing poverty, conflict, pollution and other global challenges? What do leaders have to do to respond to these massive tasks?

From military to business, from Ivy League universities to medical schools, we teach capabilities but seldom develop capacity and advanced thinking processes for the unknown. For those who want to lead for the future, this book demonstrates, through important insights and case-studies,

that we need to go out on a limb, extend our intuition and defy the status quo—even from centuries-old teachings—in order to get the best results from ourselves and our peers.
Eduardo Lovo, MD
Neurosurgeon, Medical Director of the International Cancer Center. El Salvador.
Aspen Global Leadership Network/Central American Leadership Initiative Fellow

J.C. Glick and Sarah Ngu have written a compelling and timely book that offers practical advice for building leaders capable of responding to the complex array of challenges facing this nation. The authors use a variety of fascinating examples to demonstrate that the best way to foster leadership is to empower individuals to think on their feet and react in a creative and constructive fashion. It is a must-read not only for military, political, or business professionals, but also for anyone interested in achieving excellence in their chosen profession.
Marc A. Genest,
Forrest Sherman Professor of Public Diplomacy
Co-Director, Center on Irregular Warfare and Armed Groups (CIWAG)
Naval War College

LEADERSHIP DEVELOPMENT FOR THE UNKNOWN

FORMER ARMY RANGER

J.C. GLICK, LTC, U.S. ARMY, RETIRED

AND

SARAH NGU

FOREWORD BY STANLEY McCHRYSTAL, GEN, U.S. ARMY, RETIRED

KENNING PRESS
With Lightning Press
140 Furler Street
Totowa, NJ 07512

www.kenningassociates.com
www.lightning-press.com

A Light in the Darkness: Leadership Development for the Unknown

Opening page photo: Kate Waters

Cover design: Lightning Press

ISBN 978-0-9988485-0-1
Printed in the United States of America

Dedication and Thank You

This book is dedicated to every Non-Commissioned Officer I ever served with in my time in service. You are the ones that demonstrate exemplary leadership – you are able to manage the unique challenge of leading subordinates, peers and superiors every day, and you do it with an ease and ability that is inspiring. You are the example of leadership.

I would like to thank Kate Waters for the opening page photo that perfectly captures the title.

I would like to thank Kenning Associates for their help with this book and giving me a home where their philosophies and the thoughts in this book match perfectly.

I would like to thank the Liberty Fellowship and the Aspen Global Leadership Network for allowing me to expand my thoughts on leadership and for their support on this entire project.

I have many people to thank, too many to name here, and I would be afraid I would miss someone. Please know that if you had a part in this book, you were invaluable in the process, and I appreciate you as a professional, a person and a friend. There is however, one person that I need to thank by name – Forrest Lindekens, without whom this book never would have been started. He urged me to write it, connected me with Sarah (who not only enriched this book, but my life as well) and was my constant sounding board as I developed ideas, thoughts and drafts. He is responsible for so much more in my life, but he is the reason this book exists. He is the greatest friend a person could ask for, and I am so happy he is a part of my life.

JC Glick

Dedication and Thank You

To MA, CB and AS: I could not ask for better companions. Thank you.

I would also like to thank a man named Thomas Merton (1915-1968), a Trappist monk, a writer and a civil rights activist. He is my patron saint for all my writing and all things spiritual. Here are his closing words to an introduction to his book, words that rang in my ears when I was working on this book and still ring now:

"You are not big enough to accuse the whole age effectively, but let us say you are in dissent. You are in no position to issue commands, but you can speak words of hope. Shall this be the substance of your message? Be human in this most inhuman of ages; guard the image of man for it is the image of God."

Sarah Ngu

<u>Table of Contents</u>

Foreword

As iron sharpens iron,
So a man sharpens the countenance of his friend.
--Proverbs 27:17

One of the blessings provided in a career of service, especially military service, is the lifetime of relationships developed among the most diverse cross-section of Americans in any industry. In an ever-polarized world, the US Army remains America's melting pot. Desire and competence allow for career mobility regardless of background, race, or gender across our active duty, reserve, and National Guard Army force. The American Soldier fights and wins our Nation's wars over there to keep us secure here. The most sacred responsibility that an American Soldier has is to produce the next generation of Army leaders.

I was introduced to then-First Lieutenant JC Glick in 1998 while serving as the commander for the 75th Ranger Regiment in Fort Benning, Georgia. A professional relationship forged on the red clay of Fort Benning's training grounds evolved into a personal friendship built on mutual trust in combat on the streets of Iraq and the mountain valleys of Afghanistan. To observe the evolution of JC and so many Soldier leaders like him is the gift of investing in people.

While JC was learning the ropes in the Ranger Regiment, a special operation force, I could see his desire to learn the "why" behind our time-honored operating standards. All Rangers are mission-focused, completing their tasks to high standards. Good Ranger leaders build the capabilities of their small units to accomplish tasks more efficiently. High-end Ranger leaders see mission accomplishment of tasks as short-term success, and evolve their leadership to build interconnected, vision-focused teams that achieve optimal performance through adaptability and critical thinking.

JC is a high-end Ranger leader. Today the Army would call JC "transformational" – a label that the Army now embraces after years of seeing that success in Iraq and Afghanistan was driven by leaders at all levels that viewed Army doctrine as the starting rather than the finish line. But in the late 1990s and with the onset of the Global War on Terror, JC's peers and supervisors viewed his questioning of the Army systems to train and develop its forces as a less than noble pursuit.

Very early in his professional life, JC learned the most valuable lesson for any organization made up of two or more people: People > anything else. The Army that JC knew in his formative years said that its Soldiers were its most important asset, but when it needed its Soldiers for prolonged conflict, it had serious difficulty leading, training, and equipping its number one asset. That disconnect frustrated JC and spurred him to go searching for answers. More importantly, he applied the answers he found and shared them with his teams.

This book is a collection of scientific and historical vignettes across organizations and industries that reveal the essential truths required to lead and transform people into vision-focused problem solvers and opportunity seekers. These principles served JC well in the military and still serve him today – they guide his civilian career, shape his actions as a husband and father, and will continue to shape the generations of Americans he leads wherever his life takes him.

Be forewarned, this book is not about the quick wins of next quarter's financial statement or rearranging the office cubicles in a more effective manner to foster communication. The lessons in this book will not provide long-term success unless its principles are applied and groomed in your people. Think of this book as a stone that enters a calm stream, causing undeniable ripple effects that benefit the leader and the led.

A Light in the Darkness: Leadership Development for the Unknown should have one of two impacts on your personal and professional life. You will either realize that you must fundamentally change your approach in communicating and leading, or you will validate your organization's existing culture while gaining an additional resource to mentor your people.

Start reading this book now. Re-read this book again as you move up in your leadership role in your current industry or move to a new professional venture. Pass this book along to your junior leaders.

People > anything else.

General Stanley McChrystal, U.S. Army, Retired
Co-founder and Partner, McChrystal Group
Alexandria, Virginia
January 9, 2017

Introduction by JC Glick

I never thought of myself as an author. I never thought of myself as a thought leader. In fact, I don't know that I ever thought I would have an idea worth sharing with a broader audience that would warrant an article, let alone a book. However, as I grow, I have a tremendous desire to continue to serve – not just my family, my country, or my state, but to serve humanity. To my mind, the ideas shared in this book are a continuation of my service. I see this book as a forward step in the evolution of leadership in a new era. This book advances an idea, one that I believe in and have practiced for most of my adult life, but it should not be considered the final word on how to lead in the future.

My sincere hope is, even if you don't agree with any part of this book, that it spurs a conversation, internally in your mind or externally with your world, about how leadership can be effectively done in the future. I hope that you think about your own leadership, but more importantly, how we should lead in the context of our ever-changing world. Will the same techniques that worked before work in the future? How will we harness the blistering advancements of technology? Will we need to go "back to basics," or will leadership have an unfamiliar face?

I have some theories, which will be discussed in the following pages, but they are more than just theories. They were tested in the most stressful of leadership challenges: Leading Soldiers in combat. However, that doesn't make them right – that just means they can work. The challenge is how you adapt them for what you do, who you are, and the future. Better answers are out there; with the ideas in this book, let's search for them together.

I joined the military at age 24. When asked, I like to say that I wanted to give something back to my country. While that is certainly true, over time I have realized that my larger motivation was to prove that I wasn't a failure. The military attracted me because it seemed to be a way to receive validation that I was good at something.

I did excel as a young officer, and initially, the Army's clear, standardized rules were a welcome comfort in contrast to the capricious and arbitrary standards that filled my childhood. But I lived every day of training in fear because the culture in the military was one of relentless critique, where I, like so many others, fell short of Army standards. There was only the "Army answer"; there was no giving the Army the answer. Many leaders thought that by identifying people's mistakes and weaknesses, they would somehow motivate them to improve. The fear that I thought I would leave behind at home began to creep back into my life, largely due to my childhood conditioning.[1]

I knew something was ineffective with how people around me were leading. When leaders used criticism and fear to manage, I observed that others began to hide their mistakes and ceased to approach them with their questions and ideas. Soldiers became obsessed with how to avoid making mistakes, not how to go above and beyond. Luckily, I had a handful of leaders who stood out in how they took the time to invest in the growth of their soldiers. For them, leadership was about developing people, not holding them to a checklist.

---

[1] It is important for me to note that my childhood issues were the result of my biological mother. Years later, when re-united with my father and step-mother (who is, in my heart, my mother), I was able to enjoy a healthy home-life and balanced development. I will always be grateful for their love, care and guidance.

The pitfalls of a checklist approach to training and development first dawned on me when I was deployed to Haiti in 1997. As a platoon leader, I was in charge of 36 men who were tasked with providing security, protection, and support for NGOs and government operations. One night, a group of us noticed a Haitian man trying to cut and take some of the wire that surrounded our compound. We froze immediately. As part of our training, we had memorized the rules of engagement, which taught us how to engage others with hostile intent. But this man wasn't demonstrating hostile intent, although his actions did have adverse consequences for us. The Army manual only told us that Haitians were not supposed to cross over the wires, not what to do if they tried to take our wires. I eventually told my guys to scare him off so as to retrieve our wire (they did), after which I thought to myself, "Nobody in the Army is talking about this; we need soldiers who can think and adapt."

The simple lessons that I took from Haiti turned out to be even more useful in Iraq and Afghanistan. I witnessed countless incidents of soldiers struggling to do the right thing by the book, only to have it backfire on them. While the straightforward rules of the Army were a comfort to me when I first joined, it became evident that while they were sometimes on-point, they often got in the way of common sense or had nothing to say about the situation at hand.

I started asking myself the question, "How do you train people for an uncertain future?" While the way of war had shifted, our way of training soldiers had barely changed. Instructions and commands came issued in a top-down format; soldiers were expected to learn and execute. The belief was that you had to tear someone down to build him or her back up—to strip them of their sense of individuality, of any desire to have a different opinion or thought, and train them to do what they are told to do. This methodology was effective in traditional warfare, when generals in their headquarters decided the plan beforehand and soldiers were merely the means of execution.

But this method left soldiers ill-prepared for the ambiguities of modern warfare. They felt hamstrung and frozen when they encountered new situations that weren't accounted for in the manual, for they weren't trained to use their judgment and operated in fear of inviting criticism if they overstepped the neat lines of their instructions and rules. Soldiers hid under the protection of the manual and outsourced responsibility for their actions, effectively saying, "I was playing by the rules and following instructions. If you have a problem with what I did, then take that up with my superior who issued me the instructions and regulations." They were trained in obedience, but not in real discipline. If obedience is conformity to rules and commands, then discipline is the habit of doing the right thing, at the right time, for the right reason, regardless of the difficulty.

Throughout my time in the military, I began experimenting with different methods of leadership based on my trial-and-error observations. But I did not have a robust grasp of what an alternative model of leadership could be until 11 years into my military career, when I got to the Asymmetric Warfare Group (AWG), then known as a Special Missions Unit. AWG was designed to change the way the Army thought and trained against an adaptive enemy. There, we were taught that we were capable of anything, and thus anything was possible.[2] We weren't beaten down with our mistakes. We were encouraged to keep on and reminded that there was no challenge beyond our capabilities. This mindset made brainstorming, for instance,

---

[2] I had a taste of the AWG experience before in the Ranger Regiment, the Army's premier special operations Infantry force.

much less defensive. Instead of tearing down other people's ideas in order to look better, people were eager to try other approaches in hopes of achieving better results. No one felt scared of suggesting something that would be deemed too outlandish. I can confidently say that Special Operations is as powerful as it is, not because it pulls from the best talent, but because its members are treated as if they represent the most exceptional talent—and so they behave accordingly.

When I took command of a battalion 15 years into my Army career, I began to apply and build upon my knowledge gained from AWG and from the other great leaders for whom I worked. I wanted to see if it was true that effective leadership is not rooted in authority or expertise, but in believing in those you lead, regardless of whether they are elite Rangers or Basic Training recruits. I noticed that I was getting a lot more out of my people. My soldiers did not act as hapless cogs in the machine, but rather took ownership over and pride in what they were doing. They started to think for themselves. Instead of waiting for the Army to tell them how they should behave, they changed themselves.

"Believing in" meant something a lot deeper and more fundamental than shifting from verbal criticism to encouragement. It wasn't enough to stop negatively focusing on how people fell short of the manual and to start focusing on their positives. I had to do away with the manual itself and embolden people to create strategies and ways of achieving the desired outcomes. I realized it was a contradiction to tell people, "You are capable of anything," and then give them a series of steps and rules they need to follow. Believing in your people means thinking that your greatest resource is your people, and not your strategy or answers. Your challenge is to develop them so that they can come up with the right answers for the problems that they face.

So when I was selected to command a Basic Combat Training Battalion at Fort Jackson, the largest base of training for the U.S. Army, I decided to change things up. Whether I was training my guys to assemble a weapon or navigate terrain, I did away with long lecture classes with PowerPoint slides, and instead provided trainees with instructional material. I also gave them opportunities to study it, practice it, and help each other learn, with guidance from drill sergeants. I noticed improved test scores and lowered voluntary dropout rates, as well as an increased sense of morale and ownership. (More on this in Chapter 2).

I received a lot of pushback for what we did. People accused me of arrogantly questioning everything the Army does or quietly asked me, "Why would you bother?" or "Why would you mess with something that works fine?" I am not sure why I have always had, since childhood, somewhat of a rebellious streak. Growing up, I often received commands or rules without explanation, which is why I developed a skepticism of unexplained, top-down rules and a concern that they would limit me in some way.

All of the experiences and lessons I have learned bring me to the crucial question that this book is trying to answer: How do you train and develop people—in the military, business, education and elsewhere—for tomorrow when you do not know what tomorrow will hold? This book is not here to outline yet another strategy for how to adapt to uncertainty. I believe there is no enduring plan or manual when nothing stays the same and tomorrow is always different from today. Because of that, people are your only strategy. Your only plan is to invest in developing individuals and organizations, at their pace and tempo, who can figure out the right solutions as the context changes.

Introduction by Sarah Ngu

When I was asked by JC if I would co-write a book on leadership and development based on his experiences in the military, I was hesitant.

As an immigrant from Malaysia who has lived in the coastal states of California and New York, I did not grow up in a pro-military or patriotic environment, to say the least. There were military veterans at my university whom my classmates and I treated with a kind of curious respect, but also with a healthy dose of skepticism. To put it bluntly: The U.S. military, on the whole, seemed to me a historically imperialistic machine of coercion, imbued with a macho, obedience-driven culture. But JC appeared to be a bit different from the stereotypical soldier, and I was admittedly intrigued by this world that felt foreign to me. My plan was to say tentatively, "Yes," but politely pull out if I became too uncomfortable with the ideas in the book.

We began to talk over the phone almost every week. I grilled JC with questions, not just to better understand his ideas for the book, but also to get a sense of who he was and if he could be trusted. What I found was, I admit, rather surprising.

Instead of consistently trumpeting the Army's virtues, he frequently balked at how much the military emphasized obedience to strict standards over independent thinking and self-driven growth. He saw firsthand how this prioritization not only left soldiers ill-prepared for modern warfare, but also led them to live in constant fear of messing up. Afraid of their shadow selves, they rarely ever fully realized their true selves.

Although I had no personal connection to the military, I saw the mirror-image of the same phenomenon among many of my peers. We who graduated from elite universities and entered into elite companies were praised all our lives for our ability to jump through any hoop put in front of us, no matter how high. But we lived in fear of the day that we would falter and fail, or worse, face a blank future in which we would need to direct our paths once the hoops were out of our way. Therefore, we kept chasing the next accolade or achievement. We could critically examine systemic and societal structures, but we also lived in fear of not getting that good grade, promotion or acceptance. We unquestioningly pursued standards of success by which we measured our worth—and in this way, we were not too different from the average soldier. Soldiers were told, "Assemble your weapon this way, or else." We were told, "Get into this college or company, or else." Theirs was an explicit command; ours was an implicit norm. Of course, we students had an actual choice, but the perceived difference, I will argue, can be one of degree.

In both cases, we outsourced too much judgment to an external party or organization. And if we defer the responsibility of setting our direction and standards, the "Organization" will happily do so for us. Whether in military, business, education or sports, the Organization generally treats people as a means to an end – "performance," "value-creation," "high test scores," or the all-encompassing "winning" – rather than as ends in and of themselves.

The Organization is excellent at what it does. It has engineered systems, software and policies to control, influence and nudge human behavior at unprecedented scale. By doing so it has cleared land, built farms and raised cities. But by doing so, it has also built dehumanizing systems by placing its needs and goals above its people's. Of course, there is no "other" behind the Organization—we run it—but organizations can still take on a life of their own.

So what is the way forward? Not to revert to pre-modernity, but to accept what we have done and figure out how to re-humanize our social structures – the company, the school, the sports team, and so on. This re-humanization sounds abstract, but it can be as concrete as this: Instead of just asking, "How can we use this person to achieve our goals?", we should also ask, "What does the full development of this person look like on her or his terms?"

What was intriguing to me, from the start of this project, was that this question of human development was coming not from the lips of a philosopher or religious mystic, but from a decorated military veteran. JC arrived at the question not primarily through philosophical reflection, but through on-the-ground experimentation as he tried to find the best way to lead and develop his soldiers. What was even more intriguing to me was that he believed that answering this question was not just important in principle, but essential for performance. For at the end of the day, an organization is made up of its people—if you handicap your people's growth, you handicap the entire organization's too.

You can probably tell by now that this is not a war book full of combat stories, although there will be a few of those. Neither is this a military strategy book, although there are clear implications for how we fight wars. This is also not a "leadership memoir" book where a successful person tries to explain her or his successes in a formulaic manner so that others can take notes. It is a book that offers a set of insights about who we are and the contexts in which we, as individuals and organizations, can best thrive.

We have endeavored to connect these insights to multiple industries – business, sports, education – because we want this book to be relevant to the general public. That said, the fact that these insights were, for JC, incubated in the high-stakes context of warfare is, to my mind, significant.

Once JC asked me to replace the word "game plan" with "strategy" in one of the sentences that I had written about commanders setting the "game plan" for soldiers. "Why?" I asked. I had written "game plan" almost reflexively; it's a sports metaphor that has become part of our common parlance.

"War is not a game," he said, without elaborating.

That sentence seemed to contain it all—the difference between the civilian and military world, as parallel as they might be.

Let me put it this way: People conduct a lot of their work today through a screen. You might be a teacher entering test scores to calculate grades, a business leader trying to predict next quarter's growth based on some spreadsheets, or a sports coach reviewing player statistics to determine who starts the next game. Since so much of our work today involves inputting, manipulating and reviewing figures on a screen, it is easy to slip into the feeling that we can control reality through a screen—that if we just measure, track and adjust the right things, we can systematically control (almost) everything. We are aware that this is not really true, but the mediated nature of our work makes it believable. And this belief has spurred us on to engineer vast systems of scale, to operate multinational enterprises or coordinate large-scale events—until a natural disaster hits. A financial crisis strikes. And we scramble to reset.

In modern warfare, mini "disasters" happen every day. Things never go according to plan. Something unpredictable always happens. Even if you executed your best plan on your best day, the reality is that someone could still unintendedly die. You learn that you cannot control anything, not tomorrow or today, just yourself. Warfare – putting all moral misgivings aside for now – has the potential to be an accelerated crash course in life.

We try to exert control everywhere in society through manuals, strategies, curriculums, and (actual) game plans. We try to train people based on what we think might happen tomorrow. And when we come to grips with the limitations of our efforts, we can either remain in denial or search for a different source of hope.

This book sketches out the beginnings of what that source of hope could look like.

"The Best" vs. "Good Enough" – which are you?

Chapter 1 | Capability versus Capacity

It was still early in the liberation of Iraq. The enemy's conventional force was defeated, and the Iraqi leadership had gone to the wind, but some Iraqi units were still trying to hold on. We didn't realize the fight was just beginning.

One sweltering evening, a young group of Rangers was manning a checkpoint, slowly letting traffic through as they scanned vehicles, passengers, and their surroundings for potential threats. A woman's voice grabbed their attention.

She was pregnant. Driving up to the checkpoint with two children in her car, she asked if she and her children could have some water. One Ranger brought her water, while the other two stood watch, protecting this woman and her children. Within seconds, the car, the woman, the children and all three Rangers were swallowed up in flames. The woman had detonated a vehicle-borne improvised explosive device (a VBIED), otherwise known as a car bomb. The reports were that these might have been some of the first American casualties in Iraq from a VBIED. It was uncertain whether the Rangers could have anticipated the woman's behavior. What was clear, however, was that the Army was not ready for the kind of tactics it would be facing.

One of the reasons why our Army was so unprepared was that when we arrived in Iraq and Afghanistan, we were ready to fight the second Cold War. We were loath to admit our failures in the Vietnam War, so we treated that conflict as an anomaly, a war that was adversely affected by politicians and popular support, and focused our efforts on fighting a more traditional and therefore comfortable threat: the Soviets.[3] Even as recently as in 2000, we trained our soldiers by pitting them against Soviet formations and tactics, instead of preparing them for the kind of war we were going to engage in: asymmetric warfare, in which one side has much less power than the other and thus resorts to unconventional tactics. And so we shipped soldiers to Iraq equipped with strategies for how four U.S. tanks could fight

---

[3] The Vietnam War did catalyze the development of Special Forces, but that only added a new layer of agile, adaptive soldiers, without changing how we trained the majority of soldiers. We did try to be more structured in training, but we still trained most soldiers within the conditions of traditional warfare, under war heroes who had two world wars and the Korean War under their belts and who thus could not be questioned. Only in the mid-2000's did the Army start putting together task forces, such as the Asymmetric Warfare Group (AWG), designed to figure out how to engage in asymmetric, and not traditional, warfare.

four "threat" tanks, not how to engage civilians with bombs underneath their clothes, and certainly not how to build democratic states.

The fundamental problem was not that we didn't know how to engage in asymmetric warfare. While asymmetric war might be the war of the next few decades, another type of war, one beyond our imagination, could very well replace it. The problem was that we trained our soldiers against a checklist of proven "best practices" from the known past to face the unknown future. They were instructed to execute pre-written rules, ones that inevitably failed to anticipate every situation that they faced, instead of thinking for themselves so they could respond to any challenge. In other words, we developed capability – the ability to meet predetermined standards and procedures – but not capacity, the ability to effectively tackle any unanticipated or unknown problem or challenge.

The Army's capability-based strategy, more often than not, produced obedient, rather than truly good, soldiers. To the Army, a "good soldier" was obedient and always obeyed orders. Some senior leaders were known for quipping, "You are joining our Army. Do it our way or leave."

While obedience in combat may have its time and place, it also has some unintended consequences. In 2008, a transportation convoy had just started its movement patrol and was surprised with an ambush. Before the patrol, the soldiers, like any well-disciplined unit, had spent hours rehearsing how to "React to Contact" over and over again. When they realized an ambush was upon them, they followed procedure and exited the way they were taught and had practiced ad infinitum. They had previously practiced exiting through the right side of the vehicle, and so, this time, they duly exited the right side—stepping directly into enemy fire. They were trained to react ("exit right") and not think ("exit the side under the least fire"), which cost them their lives.

That story replayed itself over and over again in different forms. American soldiers, who were trained primarily for traditional warfare and its neatly defined scenarios, were forced to adapt to asymmetric warfare and all its ambiguities. Trained to react to contact, they now had to decide if a doormat concealed a bomb or a bomb trigger. Trained to attack hostile forces, they now had to use their judgment to decide what to do when neighbors tried to steal food or wire from their outposts. Trained to seize a city, they were now expected to build local, democratic governments. Trained, above all, to dutifully and obediently follow commands and protocol, they were forced to think for themselves to navigate a complex and unpredictable war.

Uncertainty is not unique to warfare. It is, increasingly, a feature of our modern world. In 2014, CEO turnover in the United States was at its highest level since 2008.[4] Economists are worried about what people will have to do to hold onto their jobs given the rise of global trade and disruptive new technology, which threatens to replace even highly skilled human labor. Educators struggle to help students transition into a constantly evolving economy. Parents are unsure of how to guide their children in a digital, social world. Our politics are experiencing unexpected upheaval across the globe. Everyone is asking the paradoxical question, "How do we prepare and develop soldiers, students, children, citizens and employees for a future that we are struggling to anticipate?"

---

[4] Sheryl Jean. "U.S. CEO Turnover Jumps to Highest Level Since 2008." *Dallas News*, 10 September 2014. http://www.dallasnews.com/business/business/2014/09/10/u-s-ceo-turnover-jumps-to-highest-level-since-2008

These are the questions that underlie this book. The
draw heavily from military experiences. But we wi
parallel examples in business and education to amp
enrich our arguments. If our ideas hit their mark, they ought to be relevant whether you are a parent, coach, teacher, or manager—in short, anyone who is endeavoring to lead others.

Capability versus Capacity

The distinction between capability and capacity is at the heart of this book. We develop capability in preparation for a known—an essay rubric, a military formation, a fitness test, or a familiar business problem. We develop capacity in anticipation of the unknown. There is no capacity without an underlying foundation of capabilities. Yet without capacity, there is a limit to what you or anyone can accomplish because capacity is what enables you to adapt to changing circumstances, to uncertainty, and to the unknown, whether in a battlefield, classroom, shop floor, or boardroom.

To concretely illustrate this difference, here is a common example.

Throughout middle and high school, most teachers taught us how to write essays based on a standard rubric of the five-paragraph essay. This standard involved a topic and concluding sentence of each paragraph, a one-sentence thesis at the end of the first paragraph, and proper citations for each quote or example. For every deviation from the rubric, you were docked a point. What you argued was less important than whether you followed the process.

Writing in a way that follows a rubric is a "capability."

Conversely, as you moved on to higher-level writing, be it for college, graduate school or work, your ability to clearly articulate a thought or an idea became more important. Though grammar, structure, and syntax were still important scaffolding for your ideas, you were evaluated more for your thoughts and ideas, as well as your ability to convey them lucidly.

Writing in a way that persuasively articulates an argument is a "capacity."

The word "capable" comes from the Latin word *capabilis*, which means to be "able to grasp or hold"; one has to be able to grasp or hold, metaphorically or physically, a particular, defined object. The word "capacity" is related but is much more capacious. It stems from the Latin word *capacitatem*, which means "breadth, able to hold much."

The same distinction can hold true when it comes to organizations. Organizational capability[5] has been defined as "the collective skill…to carry out a particular process or task that adds value." Capacity[6] has been framed, on the other hand, as the "emergent combination of individual competencies, collective capabilities, assets, and relationships that enables a human system to create value."

At the heart of the distinction between capability and capacity is the location of power. To develop people's capabilities[7] is to develop them against a known and defined standard, such as a model, plan or procedure. The standard,

---

[5] Heather Baser and Peter Morgan. *Capacity, Change & Performance.* European Centre for Development Policy Management, April 2008. http://siteresources.worldbank.org/INTCDRC/Resources/CapacityChangePerformanceReport.pdf

[6] Ibid.

[7] Tony Blauer, a world-renowned expert in self-defense, and Staff Sergeant John Wood have greatly influenced the creation of this distinction.

developed by experts, holds the power; people are merely executors of the standard.

In dealing with the unknown, however, there is no strategy, model or manual that can adequately anticipate the future. By definition, there is no "expert" who knows what to do under all circumstances, because the circumstances themselves are unknown. All leaders can do is develop people's capacity to ask the right questions that will enable them to generate the right ideas as they encounter each new challenge. It is the people who hold the power, not the experts or their standards.

When leaders talk about "adapting" to the unknown future, they are typically talking about strategy and those who shape it. For many leaders, the stuff involved in developing capacity – independent thinking, exercising ownership – are welcomed but reserved for those at the top who make strategic decisions; those at the bottom merely need to execute. The implied belief is that "capacity development" is relevant only for those in power; "capability development" is for everyone who takes orders. But this is a glaring misstep, one that ignores the crucial fact that it is the people on the ground who execute strategy; therefore, their capacity to be creative and adaptive is critical.

To push our argument a step further: Leadership is not just about the experienced leading the inexperienced. Sometimes more experience only translates into more capabilities, not more capacity, as we saw with our military's lack of preparation in fighting an asymmetric force in Iraq. In fact, experience can even become a liability, as one can struggle to break out of traditional models when dealing with the unprecedented.

	Capability	Capacity
What it is	Ability to adhere to best practices and standard requirements	Critical and independent thinking, ownership over success and one's development
Who holds power	Manual, strategy, experts	The people
Why	Because it worked for us last time (past)	Because we never know what tomorrow will hold (future)

What Happens When We Prioritize Capability Over Capacity?

Near the end of the 2015 Super Bowl, the Seattle Seahawks, seeking to win a second consecutive championship, found themselves inches from the goal line with enough time remaining for at least two more plays. The Seahawks' Marshawn Lynch, arguably the most effective short yardage rusher in the National Football League, was enjoying an outstanding game. The Seahawks, however, opted to pass the ball to a wide receiver rather than let Marshawn run the ball, following a standard procedure that said that one ought to pass if the defense is anticipating a run. They were focused on executing according to the strategy and following a "known solution," instead of betting on the player who had consistently shown a capacity to do much more than execute standard plays.[8] The pass was intercepted in the end-zone, and the championship slipped out of the Seahawks' hands.

The pitfalls of prioritizing the "system" or "strategy" over the individual play out in many different contexts. For instance, today most people know "Xerox" as a company that sells

[8] It could be argued that Lynch's performance was declining in the last quarter, and that since the Seahawks had made it all the way to the goal line mostly through the air, the Seahawks did make the right call. We'll leave it to football fans to really duke this out.

copiers and document technology. But it could have become a very different type of company from what it is today.

In the 70's, back when computers were not common household products, Xerox's researchers created a "computer for regular folks," called the Xerox Alto.[9] It had many of the features of today's personal computer: email, icons, mouse, removable storage, and so on. But Xerox didn't do anything about it, partly because it didn't align with their primary (and highly profitable) business model. The company even let Steve Jobs tour its research facilities, where he took notes of everything he saw in order to build Apple computers.[10] Kodak, a technology company for imaging, has a similar story. It was actually the first to create the digital camera, but it stubbornly kept to photographic film while its competitors leaped onto the digital bandwagon.[11] Kodak filed for bankruptcy in 2012.[12] In each case, the leaders of Xerox and Kodak ignored these inventions because they were simply "not part of what we do." Xerox's and Kodak's strategic difficulties are quite commonplace. In a study published in *Harvard Business Review,* nearly one-third of managers, when asked to identify the greatest challenge their companies will face in executing strategy, stated "difficulties adapting to changing market

---

[9] *Xerox Alto*. Computer History Museum. http://www.computerhistory.org/revolution/input-output/14/347

[10] George Parker. "Xerox Was Actually First To Invent The PC, They Just Forgot To Do Anything With It." *Business Insider*, 29 February 2012. http://www.businessinsider.com/xerox-was-actually-first-to-invent-the-pc-they-just-forgot-to-do-anything-with-it-2012-2

[11] Audley Jarvis. "How Kodak Invented the Digital Camera in 1975." *TechRadar*, 9 May 2008. http://www.techradar.com/us/news/cameras/photography-video-capture/how-kodak-invented-the-digital-camera-in-1975-364822

[12] Michael J. de la Merced. "Eastman Kodak Files for Bankruptcy." *The New York Times*, 19 January 2012. http://dealbook.nytimes.com/2012/01/19/eastman-kodak-files-for-bankruptcy/?_r=0

circumstances."[13] Leaders are clearly aware that strategies can't be set in stone; they need to be adapted as the market changes.

Strategy is certainly important, but the people who create and execute it are just as crucial. While leaders may grasp the importance of adapting their strategy, they may not equally consider the adaptability of their people – they don't take it all the way.

If we read the stories of Xerox and Kodak through a "people" lens, the factors for their failures become clearer. Both companies were smart enough to create research outfits to let its people experiment with new ideas and technology. But they ultimately wanted their people to focus on bolstering the organizations' known capabilities, instead of encouraging their employees to push beyond them into the unknown and build the organizations' capacity. And so some of the employees, unsurprisingly, left. When Jobs saw Xerox's personal computer, he hired away some of Xerox's top talent to start a program that became the predecessor of the Mac. By restraining its people's capacity, Xerox ended up handicapping its overall growth.

When organizations like Xerox and Kodak care only about their capabilities, they force their talent to focus on repeating or iterating off known successes. But when they prioritize capacity, people are liberated to focus on the future—see the story behind the invention of the GPS.[14]

In 1957, two John Hopkins research scientists came up with the idea of tracking the signal of the recently launched Sputnik

---

[13] Donald Sull, Rebecca Homkes, and Charles Sull. "Why Strategy Execution Unravels – And What to Do About It." *Harvard Business Review*, March 2015. https://hbr.org/2015/03/why-strategy-execution-unravelsand-what-to-do-about-it
[14] Steven Johnson. *Where Good Ideas Come From*. TED, September 2010. http://www.ted.com/talks/steven_johnson_where_good_ideas_come_from

just for fun. The scientists began to realize, as they recorded the signal, that they could figure out the location of the satellite vis-à-vis their antennas if they could use the UNIVAC computer, which took up an entire room. Their bosses not only gave them permission to use the computer and track the entire orbit of the satellite, but they also asked them if they could go the other way, that is, determine an unknown location on the ground if they knew the position of the satellite in order to help them locate submarines. And thus the GPS was born.

Because the leadership at Johns Hopkins did not prescribe the standard way employees could use existing technology, these enterprising researchers were free to develop this game-changing invention. Their inventive capacity was not limited by an organizational mandate, but rather harnessed and developed. Their managers presumably understood that the lab had to keep evolving and grow its capacity, so they not only supported the two scientists' side-experiments, but they also tried to integrate their discoveries into the strategic plans of the organization.

Organizational capacity is intimately related to individual capacity. When people grow, the organization grows too. The opposite is true as well. The same HBR study we cited earlier also found that when companies promote talent, they place "much less value on a manager's ability to adapt to changing circumstances ... than on whether she has hit her numbers in the past."[15] When organizations promote for people's capabilities and not capacity, it is little surprise that organizations would also struggle with developing their overall capacity.

Organizations not only tend to promote for capabilities and not capacity, but also to hire for the same criteria. We vet candidates by seeing if they meet the standard checklist of credentials or experiences, letting unconventional talent slip through the cracks.

Chris Woods is a prime example of the kind of unconventional talent that even good organizations miss when they try to hire for capabilities – a checklist of credentials or experiences – instead of looking for capacity. A West Point graduate, he excelled as a student athlete and later as an officer in combat, serving as a Captain in the U.S. Army in Iraq. When Chris left service, although he had no business familiarity or business education, he had plenty of experience leading teams of up to 40 people in complex environments. Chris would solve complex problems, such as conducting raids, clearing routes of Improvised Explosive Devices (IEDs) and ambushes, and organizing and escorting humanitarian aid to remote and austere locations. After he had left the Army to join the civilian workforce, Chris interviewed with several organizations, including a well-known technology company. He described his meeting with the head of the team at that company.

"He started looking at my resume and said, 'West Point is great, but I think an MBA would really help you.' I said, 'That's fair, but a lot of what I have done in the military would trump what you think I do not have.' He went on to talk about how he has an MBA from Dartmouth's Tuck School of Business and how the two guys who work for him went to Wharton and Harvard Business School, and how he does not think that I would be able to add value without that extra level of education. He did not ask any questions about how I managed projects or people, even though the position involved managing a couple of individuals. He never checked my capacity in that area; he just zeroed in on a single fact in my background to make a decision about my ability to add value to the organization."

The interviewer could not see past the checklist of credentials that Chris had to have. He was doing what many of us do, whether in business, parenting or the military: We believe that how we got to where we are should be the path that others follow. What worked for us must work for others, regardless of changing environments and requirements. It is a risk-minimizing move, but by doing so we risk missing out on key talent and opportunities, as well as lower the ceiling of an organization's capacity for innovation.

After that interview, Chris decided that he would not work for this team. Two weeks later, he received an offer from Blackstone, one of the world's leading investment and advisory firms. He helped manage the global client operations team (13 people) within the global hedge funds solutions business, which grew from managing 27 to 67 billion dollars and increased headcount from 120 to over 280 people over six years.

A few years ago, Blackstone's Charitable Initiatives Foundation asked him if he would want to join the CEO in flying to the White House to kick off Blackstone's commitment to hiring veterans in the workplace, as part of Michelle Obama's Joining Forces Initiative. The Foundation knew Chris due to his involvement in Blackstone's charity events and knew that he had personally raised tens of thousands of dollars for veterans on his own time.

"Within a month or two of that trip," Chris said, "I'm pitching the CEO on creating a Military Internship Program that helps Blackstone follow through on our commitment to hire veterans. This program includes how we can help them transition from the military, gain professional skills training, put together their resumes, and so on."

In gaining support for the internship program, Chris was not trying to appeal to his colleagues' sympathy, but rather to convince them of the value-add to Blackstone. "Folks in the military are paid to make quick decisions in adverse situations," he said. "They have to think outside the box beyond preconceived notions about what right looks like. They will bring a unique perspective and skillset."

He did not pitch his colleagues on the veterans' financial capabilities (usually they had none), but rather their capacity to think creatively and lead amidst ambiguity, an ability that transcends the particular context of war. Blackstone launched its military internship program within that same year (2013) and has gone through many iterations of it since then. Quite a few veterans have already been hired.

The myopic preoccupation with capabilities over capacity can also be found in education. There are exceptions to the rule, of course. In Chapter Four, we tell a few stories of teachers and schools that build capacity well. But overall, despite the fact that the education sector is inherently much more about human development than other sectors, educators can still end up focusing excessively on training students to meet certain standards, while neglecting other areas of development.

Part of the reason is the nature of our public education system's structure and rigid requirements. But it's not just about our K-12 system. It's also about colleges and universities. Today, many high school students privileged enough to apply for college are encouraged to pad their college applications with extracurricular activities that they may not even be interested in, just to make themselves more attractive to college admission panels.

A private high school student, with a 3.6 GPA and many AP classes, was once advised, "Oh, no. You don't have a club on your record. No college will look at you. You need to join a club. How about the cooking club?" This student was already playing two sports as a varsity athlete and team captain, in addition to serving in various community projects. The advice that this student received was not geared towards building well-rounded individuals with capacity, but rather towards hitting a checklist that encourages tasks, not experiences. If this advice was truly correct, then our colleges are in trouble because they are looking for capabilities rather than capacities (more on this at the end of this chapter).

Our education system is churning out students who can pass standardized tests but who are unprepared for the demands of our tech-driven, globalized economy, one in which robots are predicted to take over many of our skilled jobs, even cognitive ones.[16] In a 2016 survey conducted by the World Economic Forum, the top three skills that people will need in 2020, according to chief human resources and strategy officers, are "complex problem solving, critical thinking, and creativity."[17] In other words, the future workplace – nay, the current workplace – demands capacity, not capability. If only we could actually start hiring and teaching for it.

The constraints of our education system are not isolated to the United States. Consider this story from the UK.

---

[16] Erik Brynjolfsson and Andrew Mcafee. *The Second Machine Age: Work, Progress, and Prosperity in a Time of Brilliant Technologies.* New York: W.W. Norton & Company, 2014.

[17] Alex Gray. "The 10 Skills You Need to Know to Thrive in the Fourth Industrial Revolution." *World Economic Forum*, 19 January 2016. https://www.weforum.org/agenda/2016/01/the-10-skills-you-need-to-thrive-in-the-fourth-industrial-revolution

It was the 1960's. The headmaster of Stowe School, an independent boarding school in England, called in a teenage boy, Rich, to have a conversation about his poor academic performance and consistent neglect of assigned schoolwork. Rich was spending most of his time chasing a seemingly ill-advised and youthful pursuit of launching and running a magazine geared towards young people. The headmaster told him, "You can either run your magazine, or you can do your schoolwork – you can't do both. So you've got to decide whether you want to stay at the school or not."[18]

Rich, who most of us know as the business mogul Sir Richard Branson, chose to drop out of school and went on to found one of the most successful companies in the world, Virgin Group. Looking back, Sir Richard believes that students shouldn't always have to choose between starting their company or staying in school.

"When Larry Page came up with the idea of Google he left university early to do it. When Steve Jobs came up with the idea of Apple he had to leave university to do it," Sir Richard said. "But I think what you ideally need to do is encourage these people – or some of them anyway – to stay within the confines of the university and get help."

The headmaster was more preoccupied with Sir Richard's failure to develop certain academic capabilities than his budding entrepreneurial capacity. Sir Richard was ultimately undeterred, but another student in his shoes may very well have been. How many creative or business geniuses have educators discouraged over the years by insisting on following the rules of education

---

[18] Andrew Marszal. "Sir Richard Branson: I Would Love to Have Gone to University." *The Telegraph*, 3 June 2013.
http://www.telegraph.co.uk/education/universityeducation/10095581/Sir-Richard-Branson-I-would-love-to-have-gone-to-university.html

rather than investing in students' creative and entrepreneurial capacity?

This is not an argument for a "practical business" education over a liberal arts education, but rather a proposal to develop an education system that is bound only by the student's ability and not by a curriculum or instructor. In this way we can truly empower our future generations to adapt, lead, and innovate in ways that will break from the rules of the past.

It seems like Sir Richard understands this. In an interview with *Forbes*, he described his leadership style as a "rule-breaker—I never learned the rules in the first place."[19] Instead of hiring for top grades or qualifications, Virgin Group focuses on hiring people with "broad experience and a wonderful personality," as they like to take chances on people with "transferable skills" who can offer "a new level of understanding to the role."[20]
Once people are hired, he believes that it is important to let "people run with their ideas" so that it is they, not him, who "set challenging goals for themselves, even if there's a chance they may fail." [21] This is how, Sir Richard remarks, he was able to retain one of his most talented employees, Dave MacKay. MacKay, who once worked as captain of a Virgin Atlantic Airbus, now works as the chief pilot of the Virgin Galactic, in charge of taking tourists to space.

---

[19] Dan Schwabel. "Richard Branson's Three Most Important Leadership Principles." *Forbes*, 23 September 2014.
http://www.forbes.com/sites/danschawbel/2014/09/23/richard-branson-his-3-most-important-leadership-principles/#70074e05ccfb
[20] Richard Branson. "You Can't Fake Personality, Passion or Purpose." *LinkedIn*, 31 August 2015. https://www.linkedin.com/pulse/how-i-hire-you-cant-fake-personality-passion-purpose-richard-branson?trk=prof-post
[21] Richard Branson. "Training Day is Every Day." *Financial Review*, 12 March 2013.
http://www.afr.com/leadership/entrepreneur/richard-branson-training-day-is-every-day-20130312-jz1fw

The key is for everyone to keep learning something new every day. Thus he is constantly looking for "new technologies and opportunities" for his teams to explore, even if he's "not sure they can be applied immediately." What happened at Xerox and Kodak is probably not going to happen at the Virgin Group. When we prioritize capability over capacity, we miss out on key opportunities—people like Chris Woods and Sir Richard—as well as breakthrough inventions such as the personal computer or the digital camera.

At best, a capability-mindset leads to mediocre organizations that may be "good enough," but can only be as good as their rules, procedures, and standards; they will never be as good as their people's potential. Part of the reason is that people fear trying something new and failing. A recent study of 8,000 managers in 30 different industries found that half of them "believe that their careers would suffer if they pursued, but failed at novel opportunities or innovations."[22] "Good enough" organizations may ensure a baseline of conduct, but their people will hardly feel motivated to do anything more than what they are expressly told to do. Capacity gets you to "better" and, at any given moment in a person's development, to "best."

The Dangers of Capability-Mindset

So far, we've highlighted the strategic and talent opportunities that capability-organizations miss out on. But the consequences of a capability-mindset can be much more severe.

If capacity-organizations place power in the hands of people, capability-organizations place power in the system – the rules,

---

[22] Donald Sull, Rebecca Homkes, and Charles Sull. "Why Strategy Execution Unravels – And What to Do About It." *Harvard Business Review*, March 2015. https://hbr.org/2015/03/why-strategy-execution-unravelsand-what-to-do-about-it

plans and models that people have to follow. We have discussed organizations that were too beholden to business models, interviewers to professional checklists, and headmasters to school requirements. But some capability-organizations go a step further: They place power not just in the rules and orders, but also in the people who shape them. They enable a fearful, obedient environment, one that can have disastrous consequences.

Staff Sergeant John Wood is an Infantry Noncommissioned Officer, who served in combat with both the elite 2nd Ranger Battalion and the world famous 82nd Airborne Division during his 12 years of military service. He joined the military in 2003 after high school, inspired by footage of soldiers around his age jumping out of planes into Iraq a few weeks after 9/11. To John, who grew up in an erratic home where he felt like he was always walking on eggshells, the military seemed like a good opportunity to leave home, strike out independently without relying on parental financial support, and make a difference.

The first month of Basic Training was a shock to him. The culture of the Army seemed no different from the culture of his home. "The whole military has a culture of criticism, which breeds a culture of fear. Leaders feel like they are on parole; any minute they screw up, they are going to get fired, and their life is over," he said.

He felt like he had made the biggest mistake. But things got better. The Army's standards and expectations were, at least, fairly predictable, and once he got adjusted, he began to perform accordingly and rise up the ranks. Still, he was aware of the enormous consequence of the Army's constant emphasis on meeting the right standards:

> "The biggest thing that fear and criticism do is they cause you to internalize self-doubt and limit your thinking. You are just worried about what is going to get you in trouble from higher-ups. People get promoted because they play the game; they do what they are told, shut up, and move along… The Army wonders why 22 guys a day blow their brains out. It is because the Army has a zero-defect mentality instead of a forward-progress mentality."[23]

While John's experience is not everyone's in the military, many service members – no matter what their rank– offer similar descriptions of the military's culture and its pressure to perform. This culture plays out in numerous ways. In Basic Training, Company Commanders graduate trainees whom they don't think are ready because of pressure from above to hit expected graduation numbers. In combat, soldiers, while being shot at, ask their superiors if they have permission to shoot back. Some leaders are too scared to tell their superiors that their orders are unrealistic and force their men to follow them at the cost of their lives.[24] It is a culture of fearful obedience, plain and simple.

When people are treated not as owners of their development, but as passive executors of seemingly arbitrary standards, then their mindset shifts from proactive initiative to self-protective

---

[23] Though these suicides have many causes, we can't help but see John's point that the Army's intolerance of failure may have an impact on these statistics. For more precise statistics, see Leo Shine III and Patricia Kime. "New VA Study Finds 20 Veterans Commit Suicide Each Day." *Military Times*, 7July 2016. http://www.militarytimes.com/story/veterans/2016/07/07/va-suicide-20-daily-research/86788332/.

[24] All of these examples are actual events that happened. A note on the last example about soldiers being afraid to tell their superiors to revise their orders: Successful leaders do trust the person on the ground to override their orders, since that person has the most information.

risk-aversion. This obedient mindset can enable not only self-doubt and poor decisions, but also real human abuses.

Unlike John, Staff Sergeant Staci Sargent (not a typo, this is her real name) had a less traditional route into the Army. She worked on English language solutions and mobile apps in China for high schools and universities for many years, before returning to the States to figure out her next career move. When Staci found out that her brother had committed to joining the Army but had to back out for personal reasons, she felt that she had to join the Army in her brother's stead to fulfill her family's obligation to the military. At the age of 27, she trained and became an enlisted soldier, serving as a drill sergeant at Fort Jackson and as a victim advocate as part of the military's sexual assault and prevention program.

She highlights the dangers of an obedient mindset in this way:

> "If you create a soldier that is completely based on obedience, that's how you get Abu Ghraib. You get into this groupthink, and you see these junior enlisted soldiers abusing someone. But you think, 'They are superior to me. How do I tell them, 'No, this should not be happening'?' That is where it becomes so important that as a soldier, you learn that you can think for yourself and speak out, to put your foot down and say, 'This is not what the Army is about.' You have to teach them if something wrong happens – especially with sexual assault – you have the responsibility to say no and stop it. This is where the obedient soldier is such a dangerous thing."

One could say, "Sexual assault or abuse goes against the Army code of conduct, so what else can the Army do beyond its standard training to prevent these incidents?" That may be so, but if soldiers are conditioned to never contradict their superiors and are rarely encouraged to make their own judgments, it is not difficult to see how soldiers would find it hard to speak out even when the issue at stake is morally black-and-white.

It's easy to think that fearful, compliant culture is unique to the military, but, in fact, many organizations struggle with it. In 2009, the Federal Reserve Bank of New York commissioned a secret investigation to find out why it had missed the signs of the financial crisis. The investigation uncovered that it had "a culture that is too risk-averse to respond quickly and flexibly to new challenges." The report noted that "officers are intensely deferential to their superiors, similar to an army": Many people "saw issues but did not respond" as they were afraid to speak up.[25] One interviewee said, "Grow up in this culture and you learn that small mistakes are not tolerated." Another responded to a question from an interviewer, "Until I know what my boss thinks, I'm not going to tell you." (These quotes eerily echo John Wood's description of military culture.) To prevent the next financial crisis, the leaders of the report urged the New York Federal Reserve Bank to hire experts who were "unafraid of speaking out" and for managers to evaluate employees based on "willingness to contradict me" or "thinking outside the box."

Not all capability-based cultures, of course, lead to crises and disasters. But these stories and interviews illustrate what can happen when organizations rob people of the opportunity to take ownership over their jobs and exercise their judgment, and place power instead in the hands of 'experts,' or those who are in charge, who set the rules or norms for everyone else to follow.

---

[25] Jake Bernstein. "Inside the New York Fed: Secret Recordings and a Culture Clash." *ProPublica*, 10 September 2009. https://www.propublica.org/documents/item/1303305-2009-08-18-frbny-report-on-systemic-risk-and.html

Given the importance of developing capacity and not just capability, the next question is, "What does that look like?" There is no "how to" or "step by step" implementation to follow because you are dealing with people, but there are some basic principles that can set you on the right path which we will detail in the next chapter. But first, here is a story that exemplifies a capacity-building mindset.

Basic Combat Training -- A Lesson in Capacity-Building

Let's return to Staff Sergeant Staci Sargent. She was first introduced to the importance of building capacity in 2013 when she served as a drill sergeant to the 2nd Battalion of the 39th Infantry Regiment at Fort Jackson, South Carolina, the U.S. Army's largest training base. In her role as a drill sergeant, Staci expected to follow the standard Basic Training manual to learn how to train her soldiers. After all, the Army has been training soldiers for hundreds of years and has created manuals and policies based on what they've learned works. Basic Training involves developing a litany of capabilities: land navigation, marksmanship, physical training, movement techniques, and so on.

When she arrived at 2-39, she was surprised that she, along with other drill sergeants, was asked to use the manual not as a set of instructions, but as a guide. They were tasked with using their creativity, experience, intelligence and imagination to create real-life scenarios that forced soldiers to utilize and integrate all the right capabilities in order to increase their overall capacity. Moreover, drill sergeants were directly responsible for the results of the trainees; they couldn't hide behind a chain of command.
"It was always made clear to us that we, the drill sergeants [trainers], not the Senior NCOs or officers, owned the success of the battalion," Staci observed. "We were going to have to take

responsibility and be responsible for the results we put out there. Immediately you felt the weight of what it was that you were doing. We couldn't pass it off to the First Sergeant and Company Commander."

The drill sergeants had to make it clear to the trainees that they, the drill sergeants, were there to coach and facilitate, but not to tell them how to solve problems. The soldiers had to figure things out and teach each other. Power and responsibility lay with the people, not in the manual.

Staci noted, "The biggest difference I observed between our battalion and the other battalions I worked with was a sense of ownership. The drill sergeants felt that they had the power to change things. Because we were responsible, we were willing to put forth ideas and make change. We owned it." The result was that the trainees owned their solutions and the drill sergeants owned their success. No one simply followed the "Army way" – their way was the Army way.

Staci identifies a lack of fear of failure as a key reason why the drill sergeants in 2-39 felt more ownership and freedom to experiment: "We were specifically told that there were no limits, so there should be no fear in trying something new because failure is not scary. Being stagnant is scary."

2-39 ended up outperforming many of the other battalions in every key capability – weapons assembly, land navigation, buddy live-fire, and so on – and even landed a profile in *Forbes*.[26] (More on this in the next chapter.) The takeaway here is not that we should always prioritize capacity over capabilities,

---

[26] Dov Seidman. "Army's Basic Training Is No Longer Basic: Lessons for Business." *Forbes*, 21 April 2014. http://www.forbes.com/sites/dovseidman/2014/04/21/armys-basic-training-is-no-longer-basic-lessons-for-business/#2d9444022498

but that we can design capacity-building exercises in a way that develops capabilities along the way. It doesn't have to be either/or. Capacity-building, in short, is a much more capacious approach.

But What is the Real Advantage of Capacity Building?

Perhaps the main advantage of focusing on capacity is that when you are truly the owner of your direction, then it is ultimately you who set your goals, not someone else. This means that your journey does not have to end at "good enough," for you can always move your goalposts. You end up competing not with others, but with your past performances[27]—athletically, mentally, and so on. In contrast, if someone else sets the bar, there is no real motivation to shoot past it once you have beaten him or her.

Tony Blauer, one of the world's leading experts in tactical defense, summarizes the essence of capacity: "You'll never know how much you can do until you try to do more than you can." According to him, our capacity is hindered by our "limiting beliefs" (e.g. 'You can't,' 'I'll never be able to do that') and our self-comparisons with others, creating ego-driven frustration in the process.

If you let people set the bar instead of setting it for them, you never know who can surprise you. Peter Hyman, a former strategist to longtime Prime Minister Tony Blair, is a co-founder of School21, a leading state-funded, experimental school in the UK. He describes the process of asking 11-year-old students to

[27] Of course, as important as it is to push against the status quo, a part of this process entails cultivating self-awareness as to where you simply will not be as good as you would like to be at something. To delude yourself otherwise can lead to adverse effects, such as pushing yourself well beyond your limits and hurting yourself.

complete a project that would normally be reserved for older students: designing a classroom in their new building.

> "Working in teams over several weeks, they first learnt about the history of education, the concepts behind education, and the skills of an architect. They then wrote essays justifying their ideas for the new classroom; provided a budget, using a variety of math skills; created an inventory of furniture, lighting, and other items; producing a 3D scale model of their classroom and a 2D computer-generated picture. Finally, they had to work on a pitch to a panel that included me and the actual architects of the new building. We were stunned by the quality of what was produced... It made me realize once more that if we trust young people more, they will rise to any challenge thrown at them."[28]

This is a beautiful example of how to incorporate capabilities into capacity-building. The teachers could have just taught all those skills and knowledge – math, 3D printing, essay-writing – in distinct classes. But by giving the students a larger mission (design a classroom), the teachers motivated them to learn and develop the skills needed to accomplish their mission. They were prompted to think critically and problem-solve as well as collaborate, developing capacity far beyond the specific requirements of this particular project.[29]

---

[28] Peter Hyman. "How I Went from Tony Blair's Adviser to Free School Head." *The Guardian*, 31 August 2013. http://www.theguardian.com/education/2013/sep/01/free-school-21-stratford-peter-hyman

[29] This "project-based learning" approach is building momentum in the United States, but it is constrained by standardized tests and education requirements that can limit innovative thinking among educators.

All of this is not to say that standards and manuals do not have their place. They are necessary to create uniformity and objectivity on a large scale. They capture and institutionalize the wisdom of the past so that we do not have to reinvent the wheel. The problem is not standards themselves, but the way we relate to them.

We elevate them to the point that it is hard for us to recognize any good outside of them. We bind ourselves to them so rigidly that we do not know how to make decisions beyond their guidance. We treat them as the ceiling rather than the floor, creating a standardized mediocrity. Above all, our educational and professional institutions at all levels force individuals, no matter who they are, to follow the same cookie-cutter training and procedures. Standards can be comforting in their predictability, but when we rely on them too much, we end up stripping the humanity from our organizations. This establishes an inevitable ceiling on our growth and may even lead to catastrophic failures.

What is fundamentally at stake?

Our hydra-like institutionalization of standards can be read as an American phenomenon. We got good at winning world wars, growing businesses, and producing excellent students. We started to think we knew what right looked like. Drawing from our successes, we created systematic standards and criteria – formal and informal ones – of excellence and built models, processes, and institutions upon them.

These "standards of excellence", which ironically often lead to mediocrity or even sub-standard performance, have become extremely hard to change, as they are ensconced into our societal fabric and are so often simply "assumed." Organizations become preoccupied with herding people towards known and defined standards, goals, and procedures, leading to, among other things, a loss in adaptiveness, innovation, and resilience.

What is at stake here is more than a handful of practical outcomes, but rather something far deeper and more fundamental that is at the heart of who we are as humans. An exclusive focus on metrics and procedures can eat away at a sense of values and higher purpose – a "why" to what we do – and rob people of their very basic need to feel like they matter. When standards and rules are set in stone, there is no need to think and no reason to feel like you matter as an individual. This phenomenon can play out even among institutions who explicitly pride themselves on promoting independent and critical thinking – America's elite colleges and universities. They are easily susceptible to the mistake of developing people against defined capabilities instead of developing their inherent and unique capacities. What results is a culture of risk-aversion that is not dissimilar from the military's.

William Deresiewicz, a former Yale professor and graduate of Columbia University, describes students at elite colleges in this way:

> "The prospect of not being successful terrifies them, disorients them. The cost of falling short, even temporarily, becomes not merely practical, but existential. The result is a violent aversion to risk. You have no margin for error, so you avoid the possibility that you will ever make an error."

As an example, he anecdotally relays this story:

> "Once, a student at Pomona told me that she'd love to have a chance to think about the things she's studying only she doesn't have the time. I asked her if she had

> ever considered not trying to get an A in every class. She looked at me as if I had made an indecent suggestion."[30]

Deresiewicz notes that elite students have spent years "learning how to please their teachers and coaches, not to mention schmoozing with their parents' friends. Whatever you demand of them, they'll do. Whatever bar you place in front of them, they'll clear. A friend who teaches at a top university once asked her class to memorize thirty lines of the eighteenth-century poet, Alexander Pope. 'Every single kid got every single line correct, down to the punctuation marks. Seeing them write out the exercise in class,' she said, 'was a thing of wonder, like watching Thoroughbreds circle a track.'"[31]

Even though we might think this behavior displays a "standard of excellence," we really don't know what levels these students could reach if there were no bar, or if we just told them to create something rather than memorize a series of heroic couplets (in which no heroism – or creativity or courage – is required).

Both soldier and student are beholden to the institution's definitions and standards of success. Both have been trained to please those above them. Of course, the standards of the military are codified in the form of rules and policies, and soldiers are explicitly demanded to obey—or else. The standards for college students are likely to look more like a "ladder" than a "rulebook." They come with fewer penalties and thus are much subtler and more insidious.

---

[30] William Deresiewicz. *Excellent Sheep: The miseducation of the American elite and the way to a meaningful life*. New York: Free Press, 2014, p. 22.
[31] Ibid. p. 12-13.

One key difference, some might say, is that students in elite colleges are used to being praised for their talents, whereas criticism can be the main reinforcement mechanism in the military. But praise and criticism can simply just be different means of accomplishing the same end: A perfectionistic adherence to external standards. Perfectionism is, according to Brenè Brown, a research professor at University of Houston Graduate College of Social Work, "not the same thing as striving for excellence... It's the belief that if we do things perfectly and look perfect, we can minimize, or avoid the pain of blame, judgment, and shame ... Perfectionism is, at its core, about trying to earn approval."[32]

An authority-pleasing, risk-averse culture can produce capable people who know how to meet any goal put in front of them, but who also lack a strong sense of ownership over the direction of their lives. As Harry R. Lewis, a former dean of Harvard College, once said, "Too many students, perhaps after a year or two spent, use college as a treadmill to nowhere, wake up in crisis, not knowing why they have worked so hard."[33]

The pattern continues after graduation. William R. Fitzsimmons, Harvard's longtime dean of admissions, describes accomplished professionals in this way: "Professionals in their thirties and forties—physicians, lawyers, academics, business people and others—sometimes give the impression that they are dazed survivors of some bewildering life-long boot camp. Some say they ended up in their profession because of someone else's expectations, or that they simply drifted into it without pausing to think whether they really loved their work."[34]

---

[32] Brené Brown. *Daring Greatly: How the courage to be vulnerable transforms the way we live, love, parent, and lead.* New York: Gotham Books, 2012, p. 129.
[33] Harry Lewis. *Excellence Without a Soul: Does liberal education have a future?* New York: PublicAffairs, 2007, p. 11.
[34] Ibid. p. 24.

The ills of the military and elite colleges are applicable to any "meritocratic" institution that values and measures high performance. The takeaway is this: Building capacity is not just another practical strategy to get more out of your employees, students or athletes. It is fundamental to what it means to be human. To think for yourself and not just rely on a pre-made plan, to use your judgment to determine the right thing to do and not just obey a set of rules or standards, are essential to creating an authentic self. Without capacity-development, people can be bereft of a sense of purpose – a "why."

Perhaps the best way to describe the humanizing impact of capacity-development comes from Staci, who summarized her experience at 2-39 this way:

> "I was walking past my bookshelf and I saw my old copy of Joseph Conrad's *The Secret Sharer*. In the book, a young captain is charged with commanding an unfamiliar ship; he has the technical knowledge to complete his mission, but doubts his leadership abilities. A 'second self' comes aboard, and the Captain admiringly finds that this 'second self' has a determination and sureness that he lacks. Spurred by this relationship, the Captain achieves a newfound creative authority, one that extends beyond his technical training.
>
> I really feel like for those of us who took the opportunity to get involved in what was happening in 2-39, we were that Captain: We overcame the constraints of our training and grew in our ability to influence. We were, in the words of Conrad, 'a free man, a proud swimmer striking out for a new destiny.' When we left, there was more to us than when we arrived."

How much risk are you willing to take? More than you think…

Chapter 2 | Capacity-Building: The Basic Components

Before we dive into what capacity-building looks like, we should first ask, "When is it appropriate to develop capacity versus capability?" Capacity shouldn't always be the (unthinking) default answer.

Here is a sliding scale with two outcomes: On the left end is "execution," and on the right end is "thinking."

Outcomes

Execution Thinking

In order to figure out how to design an environment, training process or organization culture, you should first decide which outcome is more important. Coming to a decision involves accounting for many factors, including the level of risk, the level of experience, the time allotted, and so on.

For example, if you are working in a nuclear factory where you can't afford many mistakes, you are likely to prefer execution. You are then in the business of designing systems around answers and building capability because proper execution is essential.

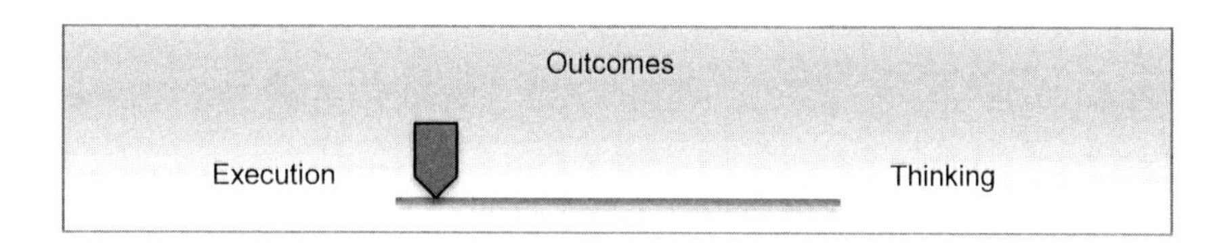

But if you are a knowledge worker in a consulting firm, you are likely to prefer "thinking," because you are in the business of designing systems around people and their capacity.

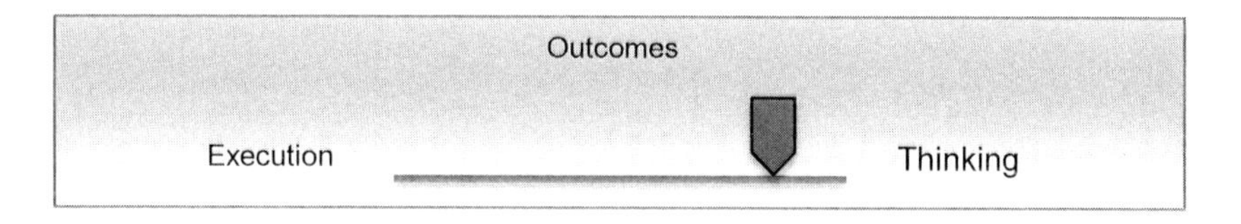

To focus on execution implies a bias towards past solutions; to focus on thinking involves a bias towards solving for the yet unknown.

In deciding which outcome you need, the main question is: Where are you willing to assume risk? There is both a risk to your people and a risk to mission (accomplishing what you set out to do). Where can a mistake be considered a step forward and not a catastrophe? Where can we allow for failure (better referred to as learning), and where are the stakes high enough that any potential gain doesn't justify the risk to the organization or its people?

These questions are not easy, which is why most leaders err on the side of caution. Unfortunately, the more cautious you are, the more you rob your people of growth and your organization of the potential to evolve.

We tend to mistakenly think that we are farther left on the scale than we need to be. We tend to believe that the risk is too high, so we need to focus on execution rather than trusting people to think for themselves. Or we believe that we already have all the answers, so there's no need to reinvent the wheel. "Thinking" and "capacity-building" are great when it comes to innovative or sophisticated knowledge work, but when it comes to foundational tasks, such as the military's Basic Combat Training, "executing" and "capability-building" are just fine — or so we think.

Basic Combat Training

Basic Combat Training (BCT) is the beginner's orientation to the military. The program teaches new recruits, who are untrained and out of shape, to handle weapons, navigate the woods, and improve their physical fitness amidst extreme conditions. If asked to apply our scale, most people who are unfamiliar to the military would adjust the scale in this way because of the high risk involved.

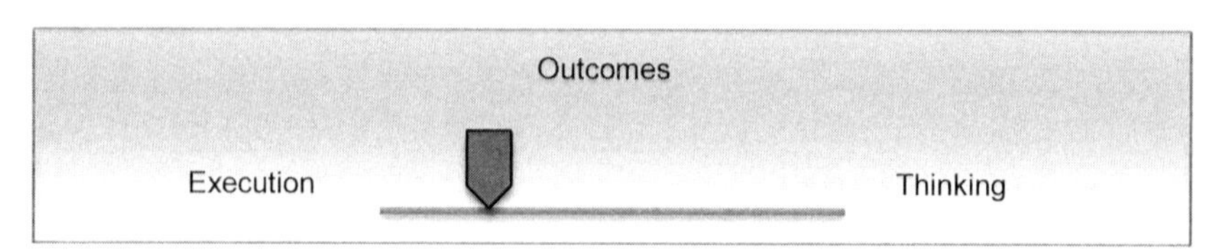

While much of BCT does sound scary to the layman, military training is much safer than one would expect. It's not safe because of its rules, regulations, and procedures (in fact, all of those things may contribute to the danger because they foster a lack of thought). Military training is safe because it has leadership – drill sergeants, company commanders, and first sergeants – directly involved at every stage. All military leaders understand that protecting people is not only important in BCT, but essential in combat. It is ingrained in them to train safely and to protect their people.

Now that is not to say that mistakes don't happen, but when they do, they typically occur because a leader was not involved at some critical stage. And certainly, some activities in BCT are much higher in risk than others. For example, we might be able to assume more risk in first aid training, where mistakes on casualty dummies cost nothing, and assume less risk in explaining the Army policies on Sexual Harassment and Assault due to the high stakes involved. But overall, the risks involved in BCT are a lot lower than people usually expect.

Now, one might say, the skills taught in BCT are fairly basic and foundational. Skills such as "land navigation" and "weapons assembly" are straightforward, with long-established procedures for optimal execution. Drill sergeants simply need to lift slides, exercises, and tests from the manual and ensure that everyone follows protocol. There's no reason to reinvent the training wheel.

That understanding of BCT is why many Army recruits currently sit through a six-and-a-half-hour lecture on land navigation, and then undergo a four-hour training session in the woods. Then they listen to a two-and-a-half-hour lecture, complete with over a hundred slides, on the precise way to take apart and put together a weapon. Lecture. Exercise. Test. Repeat.

The premise behind this model is that you have to memorize the basic tasks before you can apply critical and creative thinking—you have to crawl before you walk, and walk before you run. It's an idea that is present in virtually all sectors. In education, students have to learn their times tables before they solve complicated problems; in sports, athletes have to memorize routes and plays before they are free to improvise; in workplaces, employees have to learn the ropes and "how we do things" before they are given tougher problems. The idea is simple: Focus on capabilities first, and then we can build capacity.

Building Capacity in Basic Combat Training

The 2nd Battalion of the 39th Infantry Regiment ("2-39" for short) at Fort Jackson's training base decided to change things up. Starting in 2012 and for a number of years afterwards, they trained recruits to develop their capacity first and foremost. The aim was not to ignore capabilities entirely. On the contrary, the hypothesis behind this training-experiment was that when one pursues capacity, capabilities should be developed as a natural byproduct. Thinking should beget better, not worse, execution.

Instead of walking recruits through a ten-hour land navigation training, 2-39's drill sergeants gave the recruits a pamphlet with the relevant information. They then told them that in a matter of days, all recruits would be given a written test on the pamphlet. The first time around, only 30% passed. The drill sergeants gave the recruits 45 minutes before the second test to get everyone up to speed. The 30% who passed worked with the trainees who understood the material but didn't yet know how to apply it correctly. The drill sergeants focused on those who really struggled to understand the material. 98% passed the second test. When the recruits had the practical test that day, 100% of them passed – the highest rate in the Army. When they moved onto the next skill and went into the woods for a field-training exercise, they were already used to communicating with, correcting, and helping each other, so they naturally performed at a higher level than most other battalions.

The same logic played out for weapons-assembly class. Instead of a two-and-a-half-hour lecture, the drill sergeants gave recruits a 15-minute video, a manual, and a set of weapons, and then told them to help each other take the weapons apart and put them back together. In less than 20 minutes, the entire class helped every person successfully complete the task. Each did it a little bit differently, but everyone knew firsthand how the weapon operates.

Soldiers were asked to think about the skills they had to learn, not just execute like automatons. Both these activities were viewed on the right side of the scale:

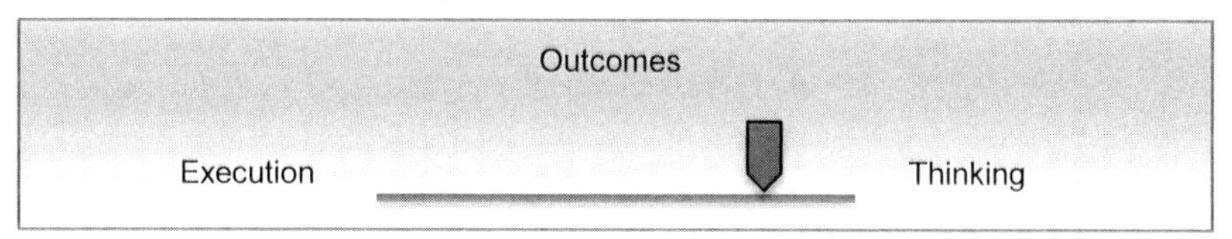

When these changes were first proposed, there were many objections: What if the recruits lose or break a piece of the weapon? What if they get lost in the woods? But it became apparent that the risk was much lower than assumed. If a weapon component broke, a replacement would be ordered; if a recruit became lost in the woods, someone could be sent to find her or him as it was a controlled environment.

After the experiments concluded, not only did none of the feared risks materialize, but the execution of the foundational capabilities actually improved. When 2-39 enabled its recruits to take ownership of their tasks, think for themselves, and help each other learn, they performed better and faster, even coming up at times with smarter ways of doing things. There was a clear uptick in morale and an evident increase in ownership and engagement among the recruits.

The improved results were not just true for land navigation and weapons assembly, but for virtually every other training skill. Trainees became much more effective, for instance, at grouping and zeroing their rifles. The average number of bullets that they used to successfully accomplish their task dropped from 80 to 35.[35]

One of the culminating moments in Basic Training is the "buddy team live-fire" training exercise. The exercise tests soldiers' ability to work together as they move into "enemy territory" in order to reach their target. Pairs of "buddy" soldiers, positioned quite far apart, have to determine the correct movement technique based on where the targets and the obstacles are located. The goal is to move down the lane towards the target. This exercise combines many of the skills that recruits have learned – movement techniques, rifle marksmanship, and so on. It is supposed to be a capacity-building exercise.

Typically, drill sergeants, positioned right behind the soldiers, tell them when to get down, how to move, and what to do. The sergeants are the real brains of the operation. Soldiers

---

[35]Traditionally, drill sergeants tell the trainees what corrections to make on their weapons, berate them for messing up, and sometimes even make the corrections for them. In 2-39, recruits were divided into pairs; each pair watched a video and received a short class on ballistics from the drill sergeant. They then had to work with each other to zero a rifle, with minimal coaching from drill sergeants. They were also given a dry fire practical exercise and their own manual to track their progress.

merely execute their instructions, because if they were to take on more responsibility, it would be "unsafe." A capacity-building exercise is, in short, turned into a capability-building one.

2-39 changed most of this. Instead of relying primarily on the drill sergeants to coordinate, the soldiers had to communicate with each other as they maneuvered down the lane. Instead of moving down the lane just to demonstrate that they had the right techniques, 2-39's soldiers had a new purpose: to get to the end of the lane in order to save an injured person's life by performing a few medical tasks. As a result, what was originally a series of tasks became a mission. And it was a mission that was a lot more demanding than the typical buddy live-fire exercise. Instead of shooting at any target they saw, 2-39's soldiers had to quickly identify whether a target was a civilian or combatant (shooting accuracy and time through the course were measured). Additional obstacles that tested their physical explosiveness and endurance filled the course.

Despite the additional tasks, 2-39's recruits actually did a better job than many other recruits of identifying the proper movement techniques, located better fighting positions, handled their weapons more professionally, moved faster, and hit more targets.

In all these scenarios, from land navigation to weapons assembly to buddy team live-fire, the recruits were not being primarily trained to develop specific skills for defined tasks such as weapons assembly (capability-building). Instead, they were given the freedom and guidance to think for themselves, work together, and take ownership of their growth (capacity-building). And yet they were able to demonstrate both better capacity and better capabilities. There doesn't have to be a trade-off between building capacity and capability. When you pursue capacity in the right way, capability naturally follows.

How do we know if the recruits were truly building capacity, and not just following a new set of orders? One way would be to assess the impact of the training on the trainees beyond their time in 2-39. Capabilities can only solve the same types of problems over and over again; capacity prepares people for any situation that may come. (In general, to see if you are developing or being developed for capacity or capability, ask yourself, "Is this skill/behavior going to be relevant no matter what the future holds, or is it only relevant for a set of particular situations?")

So what happens to 2-39's soldiers when they leave Basic Training? When asked this question, Sergeant First Class Aaron Welch, a drill sergeant in 2-39, responded, "Usually there is a big learning curve involved when you get a brand new private (graduated trainee) into your platoon. He is usually very nervous and waits for you to tell him what to do. The privates who leave 2-39 are a lot more confident in what they can do, better able to think outside the box and are always asking, 'What can I do next? How can we do better?' I have had some of them message me [now that they are in regular Army units] to say that they have completed key competitions that usually infantry soldiers take on.[36] The difference is night and day."

The leadership lessons that Aaron learned at 2-39 have stayed with him as he has trained more and more recruits.

---

[36] As context, soldiers trained in Fort Jackson are usually support staff – engineers, cooks, medics, and so forth – for Infantry soldiers, who are the ones traditionally engaged in direct combat, although now all soldiers will experience direct combat.

"I bought a wholesale of these handbooks of basic infantry tasks that are generally reserved for infantry soldiers. I thought, 'If these kids are hungry, they are going to read and learn it.' I rarely spent any of my time teaching; I just gave them homework assignments to read. I had them, for instance, learn movement formations by themselves. The next day, they walked me through what they taught themselves, and I made refinements, all of which took 10 minutes as opposed to hours."

Aaron went on, "They even made a request: 'We want to practice the formations in our barracks. Can you buy us Lego guys?' So I did, and they painted them up into roles and talked each other through what everyone was supposed to do. My kids were moving onto the next skill while everyone else was still trying to figure out what to do; they were consistently winning competitions. I gave them the outcome and the means to get there, and they taught themselves."

Components of Capacity-Building

1. Power is distributed

The fundamental logic underlying these stories from 2-39 is that power is distributed, from teachers to peers and from manuals to people. Instead of an expert, such as a teacher, consultant, manager or coach, showing others how "things are done" according to the manual, it is on the people to figure out how to get to the desired outcomes. It is on the people to take ownership over the process and help each other accomplish the goals in their own ways. There is still, of course, room for formal leaders, but they move from positions of power to positions of partnership. They join those they lead on the journey, sometimes guiding and assisting, always watching and encouraging, but never doing it for them.

In a traditional, capability-based model, people are passive executors of answers: As soon as they face a new challenge, they instinctively turn to the teacher for guidance. In a capacity-based model, people are challenged to think for themselves and collaborate with each other to accomplish their tasks. When they face a novel situation, they already have the capacity to tackle it by themselves with minimal guidance. Indeed, towards the end of training cycles in 2-39, drill sergeants only had to demonstrate a task once instead of endlessly repeating instructions to every individual. The recruits who understood it immediately would then teach all their teammates, as the entire class had developed the capacity to learn collaboratively and teach one another.

Researchers have found that the more control and power you give to people over their learning, the better they will learn. Scientists at the University of Illinois at Urbana-Champaign and the University of Iowa had 16 people sit in front of a computer screen and watch objects laid out on a grid.[37] Half the time, the subjects had the ability to determine the pace at which they examined the objects; the other half of the time, they watched a replay of someone else determining the pace. When they controlled their own experience, the subjects had a 23% improvement in their ability to remember objects and demonstrated more coordination between the hippocampus (involved in spatial navigation) and the other parts of the brain involved in learning. When people take control over their learning, they learn better. Thinking begets better execution.

[37] Joel L. Voss, et al. "Hippocampal Brain-Network Coordination during Volitional Exploratory Behavior Enhances Learning." *Nature Neuroscience* 14.1 (2011), pp. 115–120. *PMC*. May 11, 2016.

2. *Whole Selves*

When power is in the hands of the people, human potential is liberated.

Before we explain, let us back up to understand the military's traditional philosophy of development: you have to tear people down – usually by yelling at them for mistakes they make – in order to build them back up. The goal is to remove every shred of individual identity in order to forge a corporate whole in which everyone thinks only in terms of "we" and never in terms of "I." This is, the logic goes, the only way you can build soldiers who can overcome any fear and make sacrifices for the corporate unit.

This type of training can certainly produce group cohesion and obedience, but it also churns out masses of thoughtless, homogenous soldiers.[38] While that may have worked in traditional warfare where soldiers followed instructions from headquarters, it is a strategy for failure in modern warfare, where each situation is ambiguous and novel enough that no blueprint will ever suffice. What is needed, instead, is training that enables soldiers to retain what makes them unique – values, ways of seeing the world, problem-solving styles, backgrounds, and so on – and directs their potential towards the common good.

Although Staci used to work as a teacher in China for several years before enrolling into the military at age 27, her education background was never noted or utilized by the Army until she got to 2-39.

---

[38] It is, of course, possible to foster group cohesion and loyalty in a capacity-based model. This will be explored in Chapter Six.

"In 2-39, my teaching experience was really brought in," she said. "People were asking me, 'If we have this type of soldier, how do we train him?' That was exciting to me. Even now, as an intelligence analyst, no one knows of my education background. What people care about is my military experience and if I have certain skill-certifications. When there is a need, people just plug you into that slot; it's all plug-and-play."

Typically, the military would have focused not on Staci's education background and her unique skills, but on what she lacked, namely, combat experience (almost all combat soldiers are male).

Staci elaborated, "I didn't really expect anyone to pay me any attention as a drill sergeant. I had no combat experience. In the past, soldiers would discount anything I had to bring to the table. In 2-39, the question was never, 'What are you lacking?' It was, 'What do you have to bring to the table?' No one looked at me and said, 'Why don't you go get that lunch while we train soldiers.'"[39]

In 2-39, Staci was promoted to drill sergeant platoon sergeant after three cycles. There were some protests from more seasoned soldiers who thought her promotion should be theirs. Staci commented, "In a different unit, these complaints would have been voiced, but at 2-39 they knew that the argument of seniority would not fly. Just because they had more time in

[39] When asked to elaborate on how her gender affected her experience of training, Sargent said, "Typically, commanders tend to use different adjectives to describe male and female soldiers. Female soldiers, who tend to have less combat experience, are described as inexperienced, less hard-core, and soft-skilled. In 2-39, there were distinctions between people, but there were no distinctions that were assumed simply *because of* gender. We were all held to the same expectations of discipline and intelligence. This was the first time I had ever encountered this in my eight years in the military."

service or more deployments did not make them qualified for the chain of command."

Even for male soldiers, 2-39's training made a palpable difference. John Wood, a drill sergeant in 2-39 who was introduced in Chapter One, said, "Normally, as a drill sergeant, you accept the fact that you will live in a constrained environment and hope your commander doesn't yell at you. You do your two years and move on with your life. In 2-39, instead of feeling like just another cog in the machine, we felt like we were part of a big change that was for the better."

The experiences of 2-39, which mainly trains non-combat soldiers, were akin, in some ways, to the experiences of the Ranger Regiment, the Army's premier special operations infantry force. Matthew Griffin is a former Ranger and co-founder of Combat Flip Flops, which sells gear from conflict-afflicted communities in order to "manufacture peace through trade." Today, Combat Flip Flops is thriving and selling sandals from Colombia, jewelry from Laos, and clothing from Afghanistan.

When asked in an interview for a SuccessLab podcast what military skills have helped him in starting his business, Matthew said, "The ability to fail, come back, regroup and go out and execute better the next day is something that has really helped us in the startup world."[40]

The open learning environment that Matthew describes is an essential way that the Regiment builds Rangers' capacity to, in Matthew's own words, go out and "solve a problem that people don't know they have." The capacity to creatively solve

---

[40] Beth Cochran. "Transferring Military Skills to Entrepreneurship." *Success Lab*, 11 March 2015. http://successlab.fm/transferring-military-skills-entrepreneurship/

problems is precisely a capacity and not a capability because Matthew was able to apply the same skills that he learned as a Ranger in a new environment – in this case, starting a company with his brother-in-law with zero business experience.[41]

Unfortunately, bringing your creativity to experiment and solve problems is a freedom unique to a few units, such as the Rangers or 2-39. Most soldiers do not have many outlets to use their judgment or creativity.

To explain why many veterans are increasingly becoming entrepreneurs, James Bogle, program director for the Master of Business for Veterans program at the University of Southern California, said: "There are not a lot of things you do [in the military] that are new. A lot of what you do is prescribed by regulation or by field manuals. So I think a lot of people who have that creativity then have a hunger to get out and do something on their own."[42] By valuing capability over capacity, the Army misses out on tapping into the entrepreneurial drive of many soldiers, who only get to express it when they leave.

3. *Learning is the Benchmark*

When answers aren't set in sacred stone and people are expected to originate insights and innovation, there are always opportunities for improvement and learning (even from failure) for everyone involved. In a capacity-building process, it is not only trainees who need to "learn" while leaders "show them the

---

[41] Matthew credits his switch to socially-conscious business to when he and his brother-in-law, Donald Lee, realized that the key to winning the war was through providing jobs, not through killing enemies. Poverty, poor health and education, especially for girls, provided a fertile ground for the Taliban to recruit. See Wes Siler. "Two Ex-Army Rangers Believe Flip Flops And Sarongs Will Defeat ISIS." *Gizmodo*, 24 February 2015. http://gizmodo.com/two-ex-army-rangers-believe-flip-flops-and-sarongs-will-1687822266

[42] Beth Cochran, "Transferring Military Skills."

way." Everyone is learning and experimenting, as everyone is empowered to adopt a growth mindset.

At the end of every cycle of Basic Training in 2-39, all the drill sergeants regularly gathered to discuss what worked and what did not, and why. If someone tried something new and failed, it was treated as an opportunity to learn instead of a reason to be penalized. "We didn't have a culture of criticism," John said. "We had a culture of learning. There was nothing that you could not question. It was all about being creative, about trial and error."

Staci added, "The status quo was never okay. Even if we were successful and had better results, that wasn't good enough. The environment was very conducive to change, and because of that, drill sergeants felt that they had the opportunity to change things. If we saw something that wasn't going right, we said, 'How about this? What do you think about this?' We owned it."

If 2-39's drill sergeants had merely executed the training scenarios from the Army training manual, they would never have pushed themselves to improve upon the manual and to learn from each other. They would have simply settled for the lowest common denominator of good.

When everyone, including those in formal leadership positions, treats learning as a benchmark, then failure is no longer something to be wholly feared. As Major General Becker, who served as the Commanding General at Fort Jackson, once said, "We shouldn't just underwrite mistakes that soldiers make in training; we should applaud them. It means they were trying."

When an organization sets learning as a benchmark for all people, the inevitable result is collective growth in capacity. A capacity-organization has much in common with what MIT organizational theorist Peter Senge defines as a "learning organization," that is, an "organization that is continually expanding its capacity to create its future."

He elaborates in poetic detail, describing "learning organizations" as places "where people continually expand their capacity to create the results they truly desire, where new and expansive patterns of thinking are nurtured, where collective aspirations are set free, and where people are continually learning how to learn together."[43]

Again, this is not to say that a capacity-based philosophy should always be the norm. As stated earlier, there are times when capability-building is absolutely the correct strategy. Leaders need to be sure they are accurately discerning which training is truly the best fit based on factors such as risk, complexity, and importance of task and audience. It's also important to note that the two models are not mutually exclusive.

Here is a summary:

Capability-based development	**Capacity-based development**
Power with experts	Power with people
Follow the "manual"	Improve on the "manual"
Focus on "how to get there."	Focus on "outcomes." The rest is up to you.
Fear of failure	Resiliency
Plug & play talent	Bring whole self
Situation-specific skills	Skills that transcend any specific situation

[43] Peter Senge. *The Fifth Discipline: The Art & Practice of the Learning Organization.* Crown Publishing Group, 2010, p. 14.

Capacity-based development is empowered, collective learning in a way that engages people's whole selves.

A paradigm shift for us all

Chapter 3 | Capacity-Building: The Prodromos Model

Now that we have a good grasp of the building blocks of capacity-building, the next step is assembling these blocks to create a model for developing people. There are many different types of capacity-building models. This chapter will highlight a specific model – the Prodromos Model – within the context of military training. The next chapter will examine examples of capacity-building within business and education. The goal is not to dictate "one best model," but, through concrete examples and insights, to spur further thinking about how you may try to develop capacity within your context.

Capacity-Building: The Prodromos Model

In ancient Greece, the prodromoi (singular: prodromos) were scouts and cavalry squadrons who initiated action for the army. Their name meant "pre-cursors," "fore-runners," or "moving before the rest of the army." Under Alexander the Great, their "common and essential function [was] preparing the enemy for Alexander's main attack in his major battles." [44] Alexander would send them ahead to cause "disorder in the enemy ranks" and blunt "the energy of the enemy's initial contact," thus paving the way for an attack by fresh troops. Utilizing prodromoi was Alexander's method of getting his army ready for the enemy that he was about to face – it was a way to prepare them for the unknown.

The Prodromos Model is, similarly, a way of preparing people for the future and unknown by utilizing "fore-runners" in the learning process. It is *a* way – certainly not the only way – of building capacity in people. Our hope is that this will get you, the reader, creatively thinking of different ways to build capacity.

Let's say that you have four learners and you give them a problem to solve. One gets it right away ("lead" stage); one understands what needs to be done ("understand" stage), but is unsure how to apply the solution appropriately; and two are simply stumped ("learn" stage).

---

[44] Robert E. Gaebel. *Cavalry Operations in the Ancient Greek World.* Norman: U of Oklahoma Press, 2002, p. 179.

Lead
understands problem;
develops and applies solution

Understand
understands problem,
but can't apply solution

Learn
struggles to understand
problem or concept

Traditionally, we focus our attention on the two individuals who are struggling and ignore the person who really gets it, hoping that everyone at least gets to a basic "understanding," where they might get it but not always be able to apply the solution. When you have limited resources, you direct your attention to the people who need them the most – the bottom of the pyramid — and try to move them one step up. You have to teach to the lowest common denominator. This constraint is often frustrating to educators and leaders who feel trapped and unable to push people further.

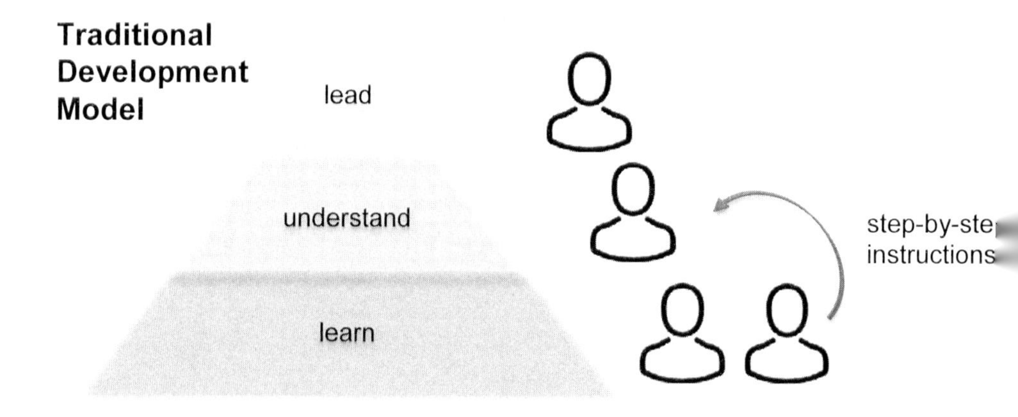

In the Prodromos model, however, all four learners are part of a symbiotic, learning system. It is not about focusing on one learner at the expense of the other; there is no explicit trade-off.

Prodromos Model

This "understanding" learner is able to communicate to the other two learners in a language that they can understand. Through co-leading, this learner will better understand the concept and gain an ability to apply the solution.

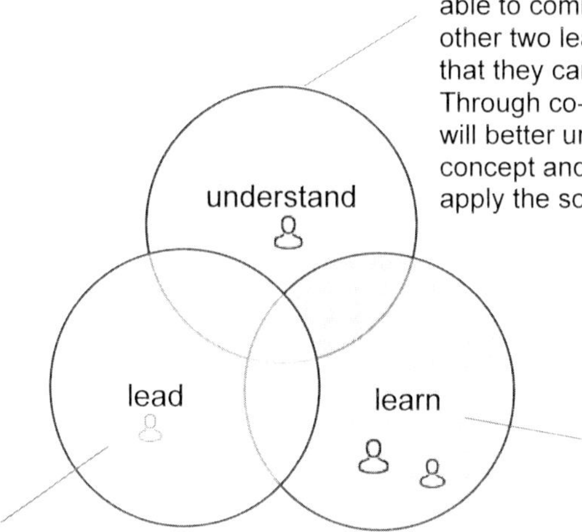

These two learners are helped by the other two learners. Since their learning isn't dictated by a true authority, they are more likely to experiment, understand and own the solutions they generate.

This "lead" learner facilitates others' growth by leading them in developing solutions. This learner will in turn grow from helping others and will be able to apply better and more adaptive solutions.

With the facilitation of the "lead" learner (not teacher, instructor or boss), who acts as a *prodromos* or fore-runner for the rest, all four learners solve the problem together and collectively grow from the experience. The Prodromos model focuses less on drilling the right answers and capabilities into everyone and more on building people's capacity to think creatively and independently, while collaborating intensively.

How does the Prodromos model match up against three basic components of capacity-building?

Power is distributed. In the Prodromos model, power is not concentrated in the hands of the expert teacher, but distributed between all the learners and the facilitator, whose job is to ensure people are learning correctly from one another. Moreover, power moves dynamically. As learners master the material and move into the "lead" stage, they turn around to help those who don't yet understand.

Bring Whole Selves. Instead of forcing each learner to learn through the same process, this model meets people where they are. People can bring their learning styles and experiences to the table in order to identify the best solution in whatever way makes sense to them. Learning moves at their pace, regardless of the speed of those around them.

Learning is the benchmark for everyone. As you can see, those who "get it" still have room to grow as they learn how to teach and help others—and they may, in turn, learn from the different ways others choose to solve the same problem. The benchmark keeps moving because everyone is always learning. The Prodromos model leverages the power of experimentation, discovery, and even failure to drive continuous improvement for everyone.

The spirit of the Prodromos model is encapsulated in the words inscribed on a skull found in a chapel built on Mount Athos in the 1700's. It was named Prodromos, after Saint John the Baptist. Christians had started adopting the name "prodromos" to describe precursors to Christ, such as Isaac, David, and Saint John the Baptist. Inscribed on the skull was the following in Romanian: "Ce sunt eu, vei fi şi tu. Ce eşti tu, am fost şi eu." In English: "What I am, you will be too. What you are, I've been myself."[45]

[45] *Prodromos-9.jpg.* Wikipedia, 25 April 2007. https://en.wikipedia.org/wiki/File:Prodromos-9.jpg

The quote is a reference to mortality, but it is also a significant allusion to mentorship and the transference of knowledge from the prodromoi to the rest of us. Alexander's prodromoi do not just charge ahead; they pave the way for the army. The Prodromos model goes one step further, as the goal is not simply to imitate those at the forefront, but to learn and grow together. We might rewrite the words on the skull this way: "What I am, you will be too – and hopefully, even more."

An Objection

Some may say that this capacity-focused approach slows down high performers by forcing them to help others, which may also affect the team's overall performance. While special situations may warrant separating high performers from the rest, this objection overlooks the significant growth experienced through teaching others.

Moreover, this objection assumes that the best-performing teams are composed of the top talent who can push each other further. In truth, as study after study shows, key to putting together the best team is not to hire the "top talent," but to build the right environment for mutual learning. When Google set out to build the "perfect team" by analyzing 180 teams, they found that the most important factor that affects the success of a team is not the intelligence, personality, or skill set of its members, but how they communicate. So long as teams create a "psychologically safe" space where people feel free to speak without recrimination and everyone, not just the "experts," is equally heard, they will outperform other types of teams.[46]

---

[46] Charles Duhigg. "What Google Learned From Its Quest to Build the Perfect Team." *New York Times Magazine*, 25 February 2016. http://mobile.nytimes.com/2016/02/28/magazine/what-google-learned-from-its-quest-to-build-the-perfect-team.html

MIT's Human Dynamics Laboratory observed several comparable teams at a major bank's call center.[47] They found that "best predictors of productivity were a team's energy and engagement outside formal meetings." In fact, "those two factors explained one-third of the variations in dollar productivity among groups." Informal coffee-room chatter, it turns out, might be more significant than formal meetings.

Based on this research, the laboratory advised the manager of the call center to schedule all employees' coffee breaks at the same time, allowing them to socialize away from their workstations. The average handling time for calls fell by 20% in low-performing teams and decreased by 8% overall. These studies show us that what is more critical to a team's success is not its collective talent, but its pathways of communication and learning.

Key Differences between the Prodromos Model and Traditional Models

The traditional pyramidal model that was introduced earlier is our society's dominant model of learning and development. One of its most common forms is the "Crawl-Walk-Run" model. The idea behind it is simple: Before you run, you walk, and before you walk, you crawl.

The Crawl-Walk-Run model was first introduced to the Army in the 1980s. Due to the successes the Army enjoyed in, for example, the first Gulf War, many industries, whether in sports, business or education, began to adopt the model for

---

[47] Alex "Sandy" Pentland. "The New Science of Building Great Teams." *Harvard Business Review*, April 2012. https://hbr.org/2012/04/the-new-science-of-building-great-teams

training.[48] Organizations train new hires by putting them in traditional classroom settings and handing out manuals or slides full of policies, procedures, and models of "how we do it here." Educators teach math by getting students to memorize all the steps of a formula to see if they have mastered the fundamentals before presenting them with a novel problem.

When we map the C-W-R model against the three main criteria of capacity-building models, it's clear that it is not well-designed for developing capacity, but for capabilities.

First, power or authority is not diffused but held by the instructor, curriculum or manual. They determine what the goal is, how to get there, who gets there successfully and at what pace. Power is static; it doesn't move from the instructor or manual to the students, but remains lodged at the top of the pyramid.

Second, learners in the C-W-R model follow a linear path of standardized steps. If you do this task in this particular way, you can check that box and move on to the next stage. This is our model not just for training but also for promotion (e.g. if you get at least four out of five stars in your performance reviews for two years, then you get promoted). Everyone has to follow the steps, regardless of how one might learn, think or relate to others. Individuality is stripped from the process. People don't bring their whole selves; they bring only the skills and experiences relevant to the generic requirements of each stage of the process.

---

[48] The history of the C-W-R model here was relayed anecdotally. Additionally, it is interesting to note that while the method is frequently quoted in Army doctrine and traditional theorists continue to use it as the go-to methodology, it is only mentioned once in the Army's primary training manual. See *Training Units and Developing Leaders*, Army Doctrine Publication (ADP) 7-0, 23 August 2012, p. 10.

Third, once you reach the top of the pyramid, you can rest easy. Learning ceases after you master the material. Mastery, not learning, is the benchmark.

	Crawl-Walk-Run Model	**Prodromos Model**
Power	Concentrated and static	Distributed and dynamic
People	Generic	Individual
Benchmark	Mastery	Learning

Strengths and Weaknesses of the C-W-R Model

The Crawl-Walk-Run model, like other linear developmental models, excels in making sure everyone has a baseline grasp of the right capabilities. The C-W-R model teaches newcomers how to learn from the successes of those who have gone before them—it ensures that "best practices" are the benchmark by which everyone is trained.

Teaching to "best practices," or building capabilities, may effectively ensure a baseline of performance below which no one dips. But "best practices," paradoxically, aren't good at helping people be their best. As Shane Snow, cofounder of Contently, once wrote, "Best practices don't make you the best. They make you the average of everyone who follows them."[49] He explains how if Debbi Fields tried to follow best practices in the cookie industry, which dictated that Americans like crispy cookies, she wouldn't have created Mrs. Fields' famous chewy cookies. If Apple had followed best practices, it wouldn't have released a mouse with no buttons, a decision which doubled its mouse market share. The list goes on.

---

[49] Shane Snow. "The Problem with Best Practices." *FastCompany*, 15 October 2015. http://www.fastcompany.com/3052222/hit-the-ground-running/the-problem-with-best-practices

Training people according to "best practices" helps us reach a "good enough" status quo, but it also paves the road to mediocrity. And honestly, this path has worked for hundreds of years. As the saying goes, "If it ain't broke, don't fix it."

But if our manuals based on past successes are no longer applicable, then we need to stop trying to update our manuals and start trying to train people to think independently, especially in situations for which there are no manuals. Linear developmental models certainly have their legitimate place – recall our sliding scale in the previous chapter – but they are too dominant and inappropriate for our current contexts. There are three specific problems with linear developmental models: They under-challenge high performers, they create false low performers, and they lower collective team performance.

1. High performers slip through the cracks

Since linear developmental models tend to force everyone to learn and move up at the same pace regardless of performance, they end up slowing down top performers. Take the example of Sandra.

Sandra has been an associate partner in a consulting firm for around a year. Let's assume the company's policy is that she has to wait two years before becoming a partner. However, she, along with her mentors, feels that she should be able to skip that step. Her performance reviews and leadership surveys far outrank most people's. She was able, for instance, to create a unique, strategic partnership between her company and a client by getting two entirely different business lines within her company to work together for the client. If she remains an associate partner for another year, not only will she likely face no new growth challenges, but she may also start looking to work for a different organization that will recognize her for who she is instead of her "stage" of development.

Similarly, the military too often loses top trainees who are simply bored by entry training. Their capacity is either stunted by the training rules of the manual, or they are ignored while drill sergeants focus their attention on the bottom 10% of recruits.[50] Top recruits, unsurprisingly, start acting out and misbehaving partly out of boredom as they don't have much else to do, creating trouble for the drill sergeants.

This pattern of behavior is also true in the classroom. Typically students who perform above standards must remain at the pace of the student who struggles the most. At best, they are placed in gifted classes or skip a grade, but they are still usually controlled by the instructors or tied to the curriculum; they can't move at their own pace. Eventually, they hit a wall, as our education system is designed for a general population, not the needs of an individual student.

In the Prodromos model or any capacity-building model, high performers can get to the top in whatever fashion; they aren't constrained by the linear steps of the system. And once they are at the top, they can grow further in leadership and insight by teaching and helping others.

2. Traditional developmental models create false "low performers"

Thomas grew up in Port Huron, Michigan in 1847. He was the seventh and last child of his parents. At the age of seven, his

---

[50] It is interesting to note that usually 7% to 12% of the class doesn't graduate at all. Company commanders receive graduation stats at the end of every cycle.

parents enrolled him in public school, but he left after a few months.

Here is how he described his experience in school:

> "I used never to be able to get along at school. I don't know what it was, but I was always at the foot of the class. I used to feel that the teachers never sympathized with me and that my father thought I was stupid, and at last, I almost decided that I really must be a dunce."[51]

Things began to change when Thomas' mother took him out of formal education and started homeschooling. When he began to receive individualized instruction from his mother, he realized why nothing in school really clicked. He learned best not by reading about things in a secondhand manner, but by directly experiencing them—ideally in multisensory fashion.

Free from the standardized requirements of a classroom and demanding authority figures, he started, in addition to reading science textbooks, experimenting and spending "every spare penny on lab equipment and chemicals, creating his chemistry bench in a corner of the basement."[52] We know him today as Thomas Edison—the inventor of electricity who amassed a total of 2,332 patents in his lifetime.[53]

Our education system had essentially written Thomas off by placing him at the bottom of the pyramid when all he needed was to learn in his own way and at his own pace. It's also worth noting that Thomas credits much of his success to his mother's

---

[51] Michael J. Gelb, Sarah Miller Caldicott. *Innovate Like Edison: The Success System of America's Greatest Inventor.* New York: Dutton Adult, 25 October 2007, p. 59.
[52] Ibid. p. 20.
[53] *Edison Patents.* Thomasedison.org.
http://www.thomasedison.org/index.php/education/edison-patents/

belief in his capacity, even though he was a failing students by academic standards. In Chapter Four, we will dive into positive examples of capacity-based learning in schools at a greater scale.

3. *Team performance is lowered (there's no time to "crawl")*

It was winter in Afghanistan, early in the conflict. Temperatures had dropped dramatically and the snowline was low. The enemy had gone to ground, preparing for their spring offensive, so targets were few and far between, making it the perfect time for training and preparation. A young U.S. Army Ranger Commander (CO) had decided to run his Company[54] through an intense training exercise to keep his men sharp before they rotated out and over to Iraq.

He ran the Company through the exercise in the exact manner that he had been taught from his early years in the Army. A good training exercise must consist, he knew, of three concrete stages: crawl, walk, run. So he first carefully led the Rangers through the scenario, without using any ammunition, so that everyone understood where the lines of fire were and where the targets were located ("crawl" stage). Then he had them run through the exercise again with close supervision, this at a faster pace with helicopters flying in and blank ammunition ("walk" stage). Finally, the Rangers executed the task at full speed with live bullets, bringing all their assets to bear upon the training target ("run" stage).

The CO was feeling a bit nervous because his Ranger Regimental Commander (RCO), who ranked two levels above him, was watching the exercise unfold. Thankfully, the Rangers were killing it, doing the best job that he had ever seen by

---

[54] A company usually consists of 3-4 platoons and 100-200 soldiers.

hitting every measurable goal in perfect step and rhythm. He beamed. Surely, he thought, my RCO must be impressed.

After surveying the Company, the RCO, a serious and thoughtful combat leader, looked at this young CO and said, "That would have been a very good exercise... eight years ago in 1996. Crawl-walk-run was good for pre-war exercises. But we don't have time to be crawling in war. We need soldiers to be ready to run right from the start."

The CO was taken aback. But he also recognized the RCO was right. The RCO had put his finger on something that he and his men had been feeling for some time but hadn't explicitly articulated. Everyone, of course, took training exercises seriously and tried their best. His Rangers had performed exceptionally. But, as everyone knew, nothing prepared you for warfare better than war itself. These pre-war training exercises, no matter how well one did them, were simply not helpfully structured.[55]

After receiving that feedback from the RCO, the CO realized that he had to change up his approach. Thereafter, the company started skipping the "crawl" stage of the exercises and accelerated as soon as possible to the "run" stage, where live ammunition was fired once the trainers were sufficiently confident that everyone was operating safely.

---

[55] It's interesting to note these soldiers were not brand new. Most of them had been deployed already, including the CO, and so they were quite familiar with the drastic differences between the ambiguous, uncertain conditions of warfare and the highly controlled conditions of training. And yet, until they received that jarring feedback from the RCO, they kept regurgitating the method and goals of training that they had learned from the beginning. "Training" was mentally compartmentalized and kept separate from "warfare," despite well-known phrases such as, "Train as you fight."

The learning would not stop with a successful seizure of a target. Once a platoon completed its task, it would immediately switch targets with another platoon. Platoons would give each other advice on what they learned from their attacks. There wasn't a singular authoritative teacher, as soldiers would help other learn, switching between the different modes of "leading," "learning" and "understanding." In contrast to the C-W-R model, those who were "leading" didn't hand down the step-by-step playbook on how they successfully did something (e.g. "the targets are here so we did this"). Instead, they shared lessons learned and potential improvements for the next time (e.g. "we should have communicated more early on").

The chain of command became less interested in whether Rangers were performing all the right steps at each stage, and more in whether they were adapting quickly to unexpected changes in their environment in a thoughtful and collaborative way. If they could do that, the reasoning was, then they could handle anything that came their way.

Moving Beyond Crawl-Walk-Run Models

Outside of the military, many environments and contexts – business, education, government, nonprofits, and so forth – are changing rapidly enough that there isn't very much time to accurately assess new risks or opportunities, prepare a checklist of steps, and slowly walk everyone through them. There is simply no time, in other words, to "crawl." Rather, teams and individuals have to figure out how to adapt quickly in a thoughtful rather than an instinctive manner, a capacity that linear developmental models do not develop.

If we want to build organizations, teams, and classes that aren't flummoxed by change, then we need to move away from developmental models that treat people as passive executors of defined steps or answers. We need to instead move towards models that treat people as agents who will come up with the right steps or answers to meet the challenge at hand. This is how we can achieve the paradoxical task of "preparing" people for the unknown. When nothing stays the same and tomorrow is always different from today, the only viable strategy is to invest in developing people and organizations, at their pace and tempo, who can figure out the right solutions as the context changes.

Beyond the military

Chapter 4 | Capacity-Building: Business & Education

We have a theory that worked in the military, but so what? How does it relate to the "real world"? In this chapter, we'll take a look at two different contexts: business and education.

Business

How good are companies at developing people's capacity—in encouraging empowered, collective learning in a way that engages people's whole selves?

Gallup, a research-based management consulting company, has administered engagement surveys to millions of employees around the world since the late 1990s. These are some of the 12 criteria used to measure engagement at work:

- At work, my opinions seem to count.
- At work, I have the opportunity to do what I do best every day.
- There is someone at work who encourages my development.
- This last year, I have had opportunities at work to learn and grow.

These are all criteria that measure capacity-development.[56] Unfortunately, Gallup's most recent report in 2015 showed that only 32% of U.S. employees were engaged at work, while 50% were disengaged and 17% were actively disengaged.[57] In the U.S. alone, Gallup estimates that active disengagement costs $450 billion to $550 billion per year.[58] This isn't a simple "make everyone feel good" leadership theory; this is about investment in your people and organization.

By and large, most organizations fail to develop their employees' full capacities. They do not create learning environments where people can bring and develop their full selves. Instead, they treat people as resources (think "human resources" department) whom they can plug-and-play, fitting

---

[56] A few of the criteria are more aligned with capabilities: "I know what is expected of me at work" and "I have the materials and equipment to do work right." Some of them are neutral or can be aligned with either capability or capacity: "I have a best friend at work," "In the last six months, someone at work has talked to me about my progress," and "In the last seven days, I have received recognition or praise for doing good work." Given this, we think Gallup's engagement statistics are an adequate, even if not perfect, proxy for workforce capacity statistics.

[57] "Employee Engagement in US Stagnant in 2015." *Gallup*, 13 January 2016. http://www.gallup.com/poll/188144/employee-engagement-stagnant-2015.aspx

[58] "How to Tackle US Employees' Stagnating Engagement." *Gallup Business Journal*, 11 June 2013. http://www.gallup.com/businessjournal/162953/tackle-employees-stagnating-engagement.aspx

the individual into the needs of the organization and ignoring the development of the individual. Instead of placing people where they can do the most for themselves and the organization, training and hiring processes have become bureaucratically focused on block checks and CYA procedures to minimize any risk that may arise.

Training

Companies too often train their employees for the job they have, not the job they will get next. If someone excels in their job, managers are often incentivized to keep that person in that same job in fear of losing the return they are already getting, instead of helping her or him grow into a more challenging role. Before long, that high performer will start looking for another job.

Even when companies try to combat this managerial tendency by creating talent development programs for high-potentials ("HIPOs"), they generally do so by training HIPOs to imitate past best practices or solve problems according to established frameworks with little room for questioning or redesigning. As a result, the organization never evolves beyond the wisdom of the past, creating a culture that essentially maintains the status quo.

Forrest Lindekens worked in sales for a consulting firm that specialized in best practices. Within months, he was selling more deals in the first meeting than anyone else on the sales team. Given the high-quality sales training he received, he was excited to be placed in the HIPO leadership campaign—only to be disappointed.

"The HIPO program was designed for the immediate needs of the business, not future needs. A lot of the basis of the coursework was historical, consisting of best practices or old maxims taught by experts[59] who taught you how to do things. It always felt like we were playing catch up; we were trained for yesterday's problems, not tomorrow's. If you got a room of HIPOs, don't you want them thinking about the future?" he says.

Forrest's experience is not unique. In most organizations, "training and development" consists of learning how to plug situations into the company's model, formula or framework in order to spit out the right answer. The assumption is that if the model worked in the past, it will more or less work in the future. Why fix what is not broken? It is good enough.

A "good enough" system is designed to distill a wealth of experience into a packaged set of best practices and frameworks upon which the organization can systematically train all its talent, ensuring a baseline of competency across the workforce. But a "good enough" system drives away the innovative individuals who want to improve upon the wisdom handed down from on high. It will lose the opportunity to learn from them, and eventually, they will leave. Often, these individuals make leaders feel uncomfortable, as they operate in a way that poses a risk to established positions, stability, lifestyle, and so forth.

The fundamental problem with leading "good enough" organizations is that you are working against yourself. By eliminating risk to your position, you are putting it, and the organization, at risk. Though these organizations tend to be too

---

[59] Often these experts may be subject matter experts, but not "substance matter experts." They know how something works but rarely why it does, as they merely repeat what they themselves were taught.

large to disappear, they may encounter catastrophic incidents that could have been avoided (See Chapter One).

Compare Forrest's story to the experience of Chris Woods at Blackstone. Chris, as mentioned before, was part of Blackstone's hedge fund solutions group. He helped manage a global operations team focused on client operations after spending five years in the Army.

"Blackstone does a lot of internal training, where I have found it to be fairly customized to the individual's day-to-day job and where there is room to ask questions, such as, 'Why? Or why not? Why not try something like this?' If the answer is, 'It has always been done this way,' then we know that is probably not the right answer," he relays. Everyone is empowered to contribute, and everyone, including the expert, is expected to learn from one another.

Most of the training occurs on-the-job. Junior analysts are regularly asked to provide feedback and input on how certain processes are working. Some business units even utilize their most junior members to pitch their business to their largest institutional clients at Blackstone's annual investor conference. "You don't see that anywhere else," Woods notes. "If you show initiative and can run with a project, and you can lead a team, there is no limitation on what you can do in Blackstone."

"That's why Blackstone is so successful," he continued. "They organically grow people in the firm rather than finding them elsewhere. They invest in their leadership development. It's similar to the military: You often first look within the ranks for leadership positions."

In other words, Blackstone generally trains people for their next job, not just for their current role. It seems to be invested in developing the capacity of its people, no matter how junior they are, by trusting them with the opportunities and resources to contribute in ways that are "above their pay grade" and that stretch their capabilities. Most importantly, training and learning happen in real time, in real scenarios, when it matters. Training isn't confined to a segmented part of employees' time; it is part of Blackstone's culture.

Why does capacity-based training ultimately matter? An organization's values, best practices or philosophy will never grow if individuals do not have the space to improve upon them.

Hiring

We discussed in the first chapter how Blackstone took a chance on Chris by hiring him, and how he started Blackstone's veteran internship program in 2013. Captain Joseph Somerdyk heard of the internship program and decided to apply for a junior analytical role. A Naval Academy graduate, Joe had spent the previous four plus years serving in the Marine Corps, culminating in his assignment as a Headquarters Company Commander, where he was administratively responsible for 350 Marines and Sailors. He had an impressive background, but zero financial experience.

Chris, who interviewed him for the program, admitted that it would have been a lot easier for his group to find a lateral candidate from another financial institution – a plug-and-play hire – whom Blackstone could spend minimal time integrating into its system. Joe didn't really know how to use Excel, much less Blackstone's sophisticated systems.

But what Chris saw in Joe was "someone with the inherent capacity to do much more."

Joe had served in Afghanistan as a financial management officer. His mandate was to manage a team of Marines and supervise thousands of cash-based transactions to Afghani contractors and other payees. Most payments were made in cash as local infrastructure did not support much electronic payments, which meant that Marines were sent out into the desert, for weeks at a time, with backpacks stuffed with thousands of Afghani bills.

When Joe first landed in Afghanistan, he quickly realized that much of his training would be of little help and he would have to develop policies and procedures on the job. Within months, he worked with his team to create a functioning system and took over another team, growing his team from six to a tight-knit unit of 30 people. Afterwards, he was assigned as a Company Commander for a Headquarters' company, supervising 350 Marines and Sailors – many of whom outranked him in both experience and seniority – by ensuring physical fitness and other annual training requirements were met. He worked hard to earn respect from his people through action instead of rank.

Joe had clearly demonstrated leadership capacity, but the question arose, "If we are just looking to fill a junior analytical seat, do we really need someone with capacity? Don't we just need someone who has all the right technical capabilities?"

Chris responded by framing the decision to hire Joe as a "long-term play."

"When hired, what a candidate of this caliber may lack will be made up for in spades down the road," he said. "Once Joe has mastered the minutiae, we will have someone who can see the bigger picture and think strategically with an understanding of how larger decisions impact all levels."

Blackstone decided to take a risk on Joe and hired him in January 2014 as the inaugural candidate for Blackstone's Military Internship Program ("MINT").

Chris noted, "The stakes were high with Joe. As our inaugural MINT candidate he would become our face of the program, and a lot of the success of this endeavor hinged on his successful transition from the military to civilian sector."

Their bet paid off. Within mere months of joining the team, Joe was not only quickly brought up to speed technically by his peers through on-the-job-training, but he also took the initiative to revamp the team's training program to better assist follow-on hires, and best prepare new members to integrate more efficiently and effectively. His revamped training initiative ended up being adopted by the wider firm and is still in use to this day.

What did Blackstone see in Joe from the onset? In an interview with both of them, Chris said, "What I told my boss when I was thinking of selecting Joe for the internship program, was that this guy can take a task without any direction and figure it out on his own. Joe was someone who looked at things from an entirely different lens than anyone we would have found on a traditional route. He wasn't afraid to ask, 'Why?' and think outside the box apart from what he has been told to do."

"Yeah that's a huge part of why I got hired," Joe chimed in. "I would see a problem and say something if I didn't think it made sense. I'm pretty blunt, for better or worse."

Aside from Chris, Joe's other interviewers were able to make connections between his military experience and Blackstone's day-to-day functions.
"I'll never forget this moment when I was interviewing. I told the head of our group that although I was …in charge as a Company Commander, there were Marines of a higher rank than me within my Company and it was difficult to tell a Major or Colonel that they needed to complete annual training requirements even though that was an implied task of my job. He related very well with that and said, 'We often have to convince people to do things that they don't necessarily want to do,'" Joe said.

Now, instead of convincing colonels, Joe has to persuade investors and third-party service providers to give him certain kinds of information. He applies a similar approach – thinking, instead of just executing the standard procedure. "As long as you don't view every problem as a nail that you have to hammer, you'll be okay. There might be something specific to that one investor as to why they can't get you something that you're asking of them. You have to think on your feet," he said.

Education

While education is fundamentally about building students' capacity to be lifelong learners, our current teaching models and systems mainly aim to build capability (on the left end). Think of how often teachers evaluate students based on questions such as, "Does your essay follow all the criteria? Can you memorize this formula or this set of historical facts?" We evaluate students for their proficiency according to predetermined standards.

What would it look like to build students' capacity, not just their capability to score well on tests?

M.S. 243, also known as The Center School, is a highly selective public school that serves grades 5-8. Its exterior looks ordinary enough – it's a three-story building with a courtyard in front, just like many schools in the neighborhood. But once you enter the building and walk up the stairs to the third floor, where The Center School is located, it becomes quite apparent that this is an unusual school.

For one, the hallways are unruly. Students are given virtually free rein to blow off steam between classes in the hallways. Gabriel Finkelstein, a teaching fellow at M.S. 243, compared the hallway to a "rock concert" with lots of people moving in a confined space, "shouting, banging" in a happy and upbeat manner. This atmosphere is intentional. According to "Basic Philosophy for the Center School," written by founder and principal Elaine Schwartz, most middle school students, who are experiencing the onset of puberty and dramatic bodily growth, need frequent periods of physical activity and healthy outlets to channel their energy.

The classrooms are not much quieter. That is because the school mixes 5th through 8th graders in all the classes, except for Latin and math. The classroom dynamics strongly echo the Prodromos model. Each class of 24 students is typically split into groups of four, with a student from each grade represented in a group. The eighth grader (the "lead learner"), with occasional help from the seventh grader, is expected to make sure everyone in the group understands what is going on. A teacher may introduce a new concept, assign homework on it, and, the next day, ask each group to discuss the homework amongst themselves. An older student might turn to the younger students and ask them to explain the new concept in their own words to make sure they get it. The teacher will then handle any outstanding questions from the groups.

"If there is group-work involved," Gabe said, "then the class might sound like the stock floor – to the point where you can't hear what the group next from you is saying. Our students become very comfortable with chaos."

One of the important benefits of this model is healthy mixed-grade socialization. As Schwartz writes, middle school is often when a student "begins to recognize a social perspective rather than an egocentric one." Older students learn to take responsibility for younger students' learning progress. Younger students, on the other hand, learn to be a little less intimidated by the older kids.

A common dilemma for teachers – across all schools – is deciding what and how to teach, given a broad range of skills and mastery levels among students. Some choose to teach towards the "middle student," which bores the students who already get it and loses those who don't. Others, as mentioned in Chapter Three, choose to teach to the students with the lowest comprehension of the material, ignoring even more of the classroom. But in The Center School's model, everyone is learning. The older students solidify their learning through teaching, while the younger students receive instruction that is often more accessible and less intimidating than what the teacher provides.

"It's not exceptional to see, say, a sixth-grader explain the material to a fifth-grader in language that is much clearer than the language I used," Gabe said. "When I was teaching economics and introduced the concept of tradeoffs and had them discuss it at their tables, it was clear they did not want to keep talking about making trucks versus cars. They framed the topic in terms of going to a party instead of studying, for instance. Students were making connections and saying, 'I don't really care if my parents get mad at me, but for you, it seems it's different.'"

Just as students regularly help make the curriculum more accessible to their peers, Gabe noted, so teachers make an effort to connect classroom learning to the kids' lives.[60] As part of the "whole child" philosophy, each teacher also serves as an advisor to a number of students for academic, social, or other issues.

The Center School's model of learning clearly gives students great ownership and power over their learning process. In Gabe's classes, he tries to only talk at the "front of the room" half the time; the rest of the time is spent on group activities, such as reading, in pairs, a selection from *The Wealth of Nations* or arranging in chronological order the events of the World Wars. While this collaborative model of learning shifts more responsibility to students, it does not necessarily make things easier for the teacher. Figuring out how to make material accessible to a wide range of capabilities can be quite difficult.

"The science curriculum baffled me the most," Gabe said. "Science is second to math in terms of complexity. It's hierarchical, abstract, and involves math. Some of my students aren't even familiar with decimals or graphs. I have to teach science class without relying on either of those ideas."

"But," he continued, "I have heard from multiple Center School people that high school science teachers like getting our kids because our kids are interested in the material, ask good questions, and are ready to learn." In other words, what high schools like about The Center School's kids is their capacity to

---

[60] The image in The Center School's 'About' page is of a poster with this sentence: "Learning is likely to be more effective if it grows out of the interests of the learner." https://thecenterschool.org/about/

learn.

Although The Center School prides itself on not "teaching to the test," last year it placed in the top ten of all citywide schools based on state test results. [61] M.S. 243 is one of the most competitive middle schools in New York City. It receives on average 300 applications for 50 spots every year. [62] Their belief that "how a child learns is as important as what a child learns" certainly produces impressive results.[63]

That said, most of students at The Center School, located in the Upper West Side of Manhattan, are certainly not poor. [64] Moreover, although it is a public school, it has control over its admissions. Although most of its students do go on to attend top high schools, one could easily argue that they are the kind of students who would attend top high schools with or without M.S. 243's help. It would be more convincing to see this education model play out successfully in a radically different context.

Let's turn to Jose Urbina Lopez Primary School, a school located next to a trash dump in Matamoros, a city known as a

---

[61] Emily Frost and Amy Zimmer. "Upper West Side Schools Score in Top 10 Citywide on State Tests." *DNAinfo*, 21 August 2015. https://www.dnainfo.com/new-york/20150821/upper-west-side/upper-west-side-schools-score-top-10-citywide-on-state-tests

[62] Emily Frost. "Center School Principal Follows Unique Approach to Middle School Education." *DNAinfo*, 4 February 2013. https://www.dnainfo.com/new-york/20130204/upper-west-side/center-school-principal-follows-unique-approach-middle-school-education

[63] *The Center School.* https://thecenterschool.org/about/

[64] Tyson Evans, Robert Gebeloff, and Andrei Scheinkman. "M.S. 243 Center School," in "New York School Test Scores." *The New York Times*. http://projects.nytimes.com/new-york-schools-test-scores/counties/new-york/districts/new-york-city-district-3/schools/m-s-243-center-school

hotspot in the war on drugs in Mexico. Joshua Davis tells us this story in *Wired* magazine.[65]

Sergio Juárez Correa was a teacher at this school. After five years of lecturing from the government-mandated curriculum, he could tell that his students were bored. He was bored too. So, in 2011, he started experimenting and reading books on alternative models of education. Inspired by the work of Sugata Mitra, a professor of educational technology, he decided to introduce various radical educational innovations into his classrooms.

On the first day of school in 2011, he walked into his 5th grade class and told his students that while they may not have as many material means as the kids just across the border in Texas, they did have "one thing that makes you the equal of any kid in the world: potential." He ended his introduction with a question: "So, what do you want to learn?"

Sergio did not get caught up with the various capabilities his students lacked. He knew that kids their age all around the world were capable of doing amazing things: memorizing pi to a hundred digits, writing symphonies, and building robots. He decided he would teach in a way that leveraged his students' potential – or capacity – to be the best in the world.

When it came time to teach fractions, this is how he went about it, according to *Wired*:

> One day Juárez Correa went to his whiteboard and wrote "1 = 1.00." Normally, at this point, he would start

[65] Joshua Davis. "A Radical Way to Unleash a Generation of Geniuses." *Wired*, March 2013.
http://www.wired.com/2013/10/free-thinkers/

explaining the concept of fractions and decimals. Instead he just wrote "½ = ?" and "¼ = ?"

"Think about that for a second," he said, and walked out of the room.

While the kids murmured, Juárez Correa went to the school cafeteria, where children could buy breakfast and lunch for small change. He borrowed about 10 pesos in coins, worth about 75 cents, and walked back to his classroom, where he distributed a peso's worth of coins to each table. He noticed that Paloma [one of his students] had already written .50 and .25 on a piece of paper.

"One peso is one peso," he said. "What's one-half?"

At first, a number of kids divided the coins into clearly unequal piles. It sparked a debate among the students about what one-half meant. Juárez Correa's training told him to intervene. But now he remembered Mitra's research and resisted the urge. Instead, he watched as Alma Delia Juárez Flores explained to her tablemates that half means equal portions. She counted out 50 centavos. "So the answer is .50," she said. The other kids nodded. It made sense.

... He began experimenting with different ways of posing open-ended questions on subjects ranging from the volume of cubes to multiplying fractions. "The volume of a square-based prism is the area of the base times the height.

The volume of a square-based pyramid is that formula divided by three," he said one morning. "Why do you think that is?"

He walked around the room, saying little. It was fascinating to watch the kids approach the answer. They were working in teams and had models of various shapes to look at and play with. The team led by Usiel Lemus Aquino, a short boy with an ever-present hopeful expression, hit on the idea of drawing the different shapes—prisms and pyramids. By layering the drawings on top of each other, they began to divine the answer. Juárez Correa let the kids talk freely. It was a noisy, slightly chaotic environment—exactly the opposite of the sort of factory-friendly discipline that teachers were expected to impose. But within 20 minutes, they had come up with the answer.

> "Three pyramids fit in one prism," Usiel observed, speaking for the group. "So the volume of a pyramid must be the volume of a prism divided by three."

Sergio's primary goal was not that the kids reached the right answers. It was that they came to the right answers by themselves, because once they strengthened their capacity – to think critically and creatively, and to help each other – then they could solve any problem that came their way. Just like in 2-39, all the students received were the goal or outcome and a bit of guidance. They taught themselves the rest.

But, some teachers may ask, how do we do this and prepare students for standardized testing? How can we innovate when performance is measured by regulated metrics? Interestingly enough, when it came time to take the national standardized exam, nearly half of Sergio's class performed at a world-class level. The year before, nearly half of the class failed the math section, and 31 percent failed Spanish. This time around, only 7 percent failed math, and 3.5 percent failed Spanish. In fact, ten students scored in the 99.99th percentile in math, including a student who received the highest math score in the entire country.

Outside of the learning environment, Sergio let his students elect leaders who decided how to run the class and enforce discipline. By democratizing power, he helped students develop leadership and conflict-resolution skills instead of always resorting to him to adjudicate.

Hannah D'Apice was a sixth grade social studies teacher who taught at a Title I middle school in Dallas, Texas (she is currently getting her Masters in Education at Stanford University).[66] During her time there, she was determined not only to teach required material, but also to "expose my students to social justice issues and give them the capacity to think about it if they saw some sort of injustice."

In addition to her required curriculum, she taught several lessons on racism, classism, able-ism, etc., and educated her students on local and school board elections and what they could do to participate. She found that the students were much more engaged with this contemporary material—they were asking more questions than she was asking them. Her students began to connect the dots between what they were learning in school and in their lives. One incident stands out to Hannah in particular.

"At the beginning of class, a black girl said, 'I want to dye my hair.' One of my Hispanic girls responded, 'You can't dye it. It's too dark.' Their peers exploded, saying, 'Oh my god, this is racist,'" Hannah said.

---

[66] Title 1 schools receive financial assistance from the government due to having high numbers or high percentages of children from low-income families.

"They brought it to me as the arbiter, but they were discussing mostly among themselves. Then one of the boys announced the conclusion: 'Ok, this was not racist. We know now you did not mean to be racist, but the way you said it just reminded us of racist things that other people have said,'" she said. "I didn't teach a lesson that day."

Her students, by themselves, reached a fairly nuanced conclusion on a complicated scenario that even some adults may have struggled to evaluate. In that moment, they demonstrated learning that far exceeded memorizing material and answering all the right questions on a test. They demonstrated the capacity to take their prior learning about racism – the concepts, vocabulary, and examples – and apply it to evaluate a new scenario by themselves.

So far our education examples are from the K-12 system. What about higher education schools? Let's take a look at Harvard University.

In the 1990's, Eric Mazur, a professor at Harvard, had been teaching introductory physics to undergraduates for several years. He had been receiving high student evaluations and didn't think anything was wrong with his teaching style, until, inspired by an article he read, he decided to administer a simple quiz. Unlike most of Mazur's tests, this quiz didn't require handling equations or formulas. Through simple world problems, it tested students' fundamental understanding of the concepts in physics—for instance, if a heavy car and a light car collided, which car exerted the greater force? (The answer is that both forces are the same; weight is irrelevant to force exerted).

Two-thirds of students scored poorly on this quiz. Eric had to reflect on what exactly his students were learning from him.

"The students did well on textbook-style problems," he explained in an interview with Harvard Magazine. "They had a bag of tricks, formulas to apply. But that was solving problems by rote. They floundered on the simple word problems, which demanded a real understanding of the concepts behind the formulas."[67]

In other words, they had great capabilities, but no real capacity. As he tried to explain the answers to the quiz to his students, he realized that he was not getting through. Frustrated, he told the 150-person class, "Why don't you discuss it with one another?" Within three minutes of chaotic conversation, the class had figured it out by themselves and told him to move on.

Through this experience, Eric realized that students can often make better teachers than the teachers themselves. "You're a student and you've only recently learned this, so you still know where you got hung up, because it's not that long ago that *you* were hung up on that very same thing. Whereas Professor Mazur got hung up on this point when he was 17, and he no longer remembers how difficult it was back then. He has lost the ability to understand what a beginning learner faces," he said.

Eric's description of the peer-to-peer learning process strongly echoes The Center School's learning model, in which older students teach younger students academic concepts in terms that they will understand. It exemplifies why students can be so effective at teaching each other. Sometimes it is more helpful to learn from someone who has just been where you are now than from someone who is years ahead of you.[68]

---

[67] Craig Lambert. "Twilight of the Lecture." *Harvard Magazine*, March-April 2012. http://harvardmagazine.com/2012/03/twilight-of-the-lecture

[68] Recall the quote on the "Prodromos skull": "What I am, you will be too. What you are, I've been myself."

Catalyzed by his experience, Eric developed a new pedagogical method centered around the "flipped classroom."[69] In this model, students read the textbook and notes before class and then gather to discuss questions. Eric begins class with a student-sourced question. He then polls the class with hand-held devices to see how many have come up with the right answer. If 30 to 70 percent of the class gets the correct answer, he asks each student to find a neighbor with a different answer and debate. After a few minutes of conversation, students vote again, and the percentage of those with the correct answers usually increases dramatically. In 2014, Eric received the Minerva Prize for Advancements in Higher Education for his "impact on student learning experiences through extraordinary innovation in higher education."[70]

"Education is a two-step process," Eric said. "The first step, you need to transfer information. In the second step, the learner needs to do something with that information — build mental models, make sense of it, be able to see how that information and the knowledge embedded in it applies to the world around us."[71]

Eric understands that the impact of a classroom has wide-reaching effects outside it. "We want to educate leaders, the innovators of society. Let's turn our students into *real* problem solvers," he said. "We have to train people to tackle situations they have not encountered before ... The first step in developing

---

[69] As Chapter Two indicates, this was a technique also used in 2-39 with much success.
[70] Julie Schell. "Eric Mazur wins first ever Minerva Prize for Advancements in Higher Education." *Turn to Your Neighbor: The Official Peer Instruction Blog*, 20 May 2014. http://blog.peerinstruction.net/2014/05/20/eric-mazur-wins-first-ever-minerva-prize-for-advancements-in-higher-education/
[71] Eric Mazur. "The Flipped Classroom Will Redefine the Role of Educators." *The Evollution*, 13 March 2013. http://www.evolllution.com/distance_online_learning/audio-flipped-classroom-redefine-role-educators-10-years/

those skills is stepping into unknown territory."[72] We would be hard-pressed to find a better definition of "capacity."

One of the most impressive models in education that we have come across is The Cloverleaf School of Atlanta. It exemplifies how an entire system, not just an individual teacher, can be oriented towards building capacity. It is a private, non-profit school that serves kindergarten through seventh grade students, specializing in educating children with ADHD, autism, and other learning differences.

The co-founders of the school, Emily Swindall, Jen Owen and Katherine McGee, all previously had experiences with schools that served similar student populations. They grew frustrated with teachers' low expectations and their comments about students (e.g. "We don't need to teach them that because it's not like they are going to college").

The co-founders were determined to make Cloverleaf different not just from the typical "special needs" school, but also from any other school. They were going to focus less on their students' specific capabilities and more on their capacity for growth. They wanted to start a school that would not presume what their students were capable of or where they would end up. The motto of Cloverleaf is, fittingly, "Quo Vadis?" ("Where are you going?").

When Travis (name changed) entered Cloverleaf at age seven, he was academically far behind his peers. He was not writing and barely reading. Because his previous teachers felt he didn't have the social foundation to learn academically (a common assumption made of many students before they arrive at Cloverleaf), they never exposed him to math. For instance,

[72] Craig Lambert. "Twilight of the Lecture." *Harvard Magazine*, March-April 2012.

when his teachers placed math blocks on the table for students to use, Travis shook the table until all the blocks fell off. When the students were making pizza and Travis was too nervous to engage, his teachers did not bother to help him finish. Given that his behavior was often either disruptive or disengaged, he was regularly removed from the classroom, which meant he was rarely exposed to anything academically challenging. Frustrated by this, his mother decided to enroll him at Cloverleaf.

While some schools would have dismissed Travis as a lost cause, Cloverleaf started Travis off with a one-on-one tutor who recognized his academic potential. The next challenge was to integrate Travis into classroom learning. Although Travis did not meet the checklist of what a "ready student" looked like, Cloverleaf's teachers knew that he had a tremendous academic capacity that was hidden, and that he likely just needed a different route to get there.

His Cloverleaf teachers figured out that his signs of disengagement did not mean that he was not "ready to learn," but that he was simply bored from the lack of challenge. So when he would look out the window while his teacher was talking, not paying attention to the class discussion, his teacher would think, "Ok, what can I do to engage him?" instead of pinning the blame on Travis as the person who needed to correct his behavior.

They experimented with different ways of reaching him. While he struggled with pencil-to-paper learning, they found that he loved learning through electronic games and apps. Out of his own interest, he completed an entire grade's worth of math in the game, Splash Math. They found that a story-telling curriculum best helped him access phonetic sounds while reading. They learned what his interests were and found books in those subject areas, which enabled a huge jump in his reading comprehension. They tried to understand and teach to his whole self.

Travis still had behavioral struggles. But when his teachers learned that he would pick up and shake a table whenever he was frustrated, they worked with him to better channel his frustration and respond more flexibly to unexpected situations. Cloverleaf's philosophy is that students' social difficulties often stem from a lack of coping strategies; they do not know how to cope with the world around them, which leads to overwhelming anxiety, rage or sadness. "Behavior is a form of communication. When we see a student do an unexpected or inappropriate behavior, we know that student is trying to communicate a message that he or she does not yet have the appropriate tools or words to express in a pro-social way," Jen said.

That was certainly the case with Claudia (name changed), who enrolled in 5th grade at age ten. Anytime Claudia felt embarrassed – when she was called upon, when she felt that someone was mean to her, or when an unexpected mistake occurred – she had a severe emotional breakdown, sometimes crying for well over an hour, impeding her and her classmates' learning. Even if a comment was not directed at her, as long as she believed that it was meant to demean her, she was unable to recover. Her teachers helped her to develop strategies to identify her triggers and respond more productively.

All Cloverleaf students receive similar guidance. Everyone's school day begins on the playground. The first class is on social skills. Teachers give lessons such as, "What does it mean to be a good friend?" and "How do we give feedback?" As students practice these skills throughout the day, these lessons are reinforced. At the end of the day at 3 pm, the students gather in a circle for "reflection time," where they – not the teacher – provide feedback on how they behaved, giving out both "compliments" and "wishes." Sometimes, they even give the teacher feedback. In addition, students set weekly goals (e.g. bring my water bottle to every class) and celebrate any progress made at the end of each week.

Within a year at Cloverleaf, Claudia was able to ask proactively for what she needed. She could tell a student, "That tone of voice is really hurtful. Can you ask me in this way?" or ask permission to type up an assignment, as handwriting was a process so laborious that it often provoked a meltdown. The biggest test of her skills came during the school's talent show.

Claudia was performing a piano act onstage with a keyboard. In the middle of her performance, the speakers on her keyboard stopped working. A year before, she would have broken down at this major, unexpected embarrassment and not been able to continue. Instead, she took a deep breath, applied all the strategies she had learned, and waited for the keyboard to be fixed. She restarted her piece and received a huge round of applause at the end.

What Cloverleaf is doing is much more than "personalized learning," although that is important and relevant. They do something more fundamental: Help students become self-directed agents in a world that usually tells them what to do.[73]

First, Cloverleaf's teachers "assume competence." They believe that the kids have the capacity to exceed expectations, but that they will do so in their own time and way, instead of following standard procedures. Teachers with a capability-mindset would automatically judge students like Travis or

---

[73] For more information, see Katherine McGee and Jen Owen, "Positive Behavior Support System That Works- School-Wide, Classroom, and Home" (2015). *Georgia Association for Positive Behavior Support Conference*. 20. http://digitalcommons.georgiasouthern.edu/gapbs/2015/2015/20/

Claudia as failures; they would try to force them to meet a checklist of requirements before labeling them "ready to learn." That mindset would have overlooked the fact that Travis, for instance, was disengaged because he wasn't reached in the right ways or taught the right social skills. According to its co-founders, Cloverleaf strives to "meet students where they are, then move them forward," instead of meeting "students where they're supposed to be." They begin from students' capacity rather than from preset standards. As a result, the question is never, "What is wrong with this student?" but "How can we help this student?"

Cloverleaf's teachers certainly teach their students specific capabilities. Claudia had to learn concrete steps and skills to minimize her breakdowns. But she wasn't taught specific behaviors to imitate "just because the teacher said so." She was learning the right behaviors and skills in order to advocate for her needs, turning her from a passive reactor to an agent capable of regaining control over a destabilizing situation. Cloverleaf's teachers try to say "yes" as often as reasonably possible.[74] If a student asks, "I'm hungry, can I eat my snacks now?" the teacher does not say, "Wait until lunch break," but lets the student go ahead and eat. Katherine explained, "We ask kids to self-advocate for themselves because you have to do so as an adult."

"When you devalue what they are interested in by saying, 'That's not what we are talking about right now,' then they are not willing to hear the value of what you are saying. We try to give what they want value by saying 'Yes, we'll add that component in the class.' The more you say 'yes,' the more willing people are to hear the word 'no,'" Katherine said. If

---

[74] This is true even in terms of the content of the education. See Chapter Six, "Capacity Building: Culture and Leadership," for details.

teachers do have to say no, they often reframe it in terms of a "Yes + a time frame" (e.g. "Yes you can have do that after this activity").

Students are asked to bring their whole selves, including their desires and interests, to the classroom table. Teachers do not hold all the power, but serve as partners alongside students. This can be a hard thing for many teachers, who are traditionally taught to "have command" or "be in control" of the classroom.

As a private school, The Cloverleaf School certainly enjoys certain freedoms and resources to execute its unique philosophy, but many of its practices can be adopted and adapted to most classrooms. It is a paragon of what a school system can look like if it is redesigned from scratch with capacity, not capability, in mind.

Values without context are just words

Chapter 5 | Capacity Building: Values & Discipline

You are the leader of a Special Operations Team. Your current mission is to capture a target as soon as possible. You and your team are sitting in the tactical operations center, waiting for the target's location to be confirmed. The confirmation comes in. You all quickly board an aircraft headed toward the target. Your team slides down ropes off helicopters to designated blocking positions.

One of your team's top goals is to isolate the target, ensuring that the target doesn't escape and that enemy reinforcements do not enter the area. Blocking the target area, however, does not just prevent "bad guys" from coming and going. You quickly realize that civilians in the area are also prevented from moving.

They want to be able to trade goods, visit people and go home. They want the freedom to move about freely.

At first, your team tries to speed things up. The sooner your team is done with its tasks, the sooner civilians can travel in and out. Your team picks up its pace, but you can only work so fast without compromising the mission. Signs of unrest and unease begin to show among the civilians, who start to treat the American presence as an occupying, imposing force. What do you do?

This dilemma is just one of many ambiguities that soldiers face in modern warfare. As the world becomes increasingly interconnected, it is harder and harder – in war and in life – to make decisions in a void without any secondary or tertiary effects.

The previous chapter contrasted "thinking" with "execution." If we take an "execution" or "obedience" approach to this dilemma, we would ask, "What do the rules say? What about my supervisor?" But if we take a "thinking" approach, then we would step back and ask, "What is our mission here? What are the implications of our actions?"

Let's take the latter approach to the (actual, not fictitious) dilemma posed above. The mission, in that context, was to secure the area and find the target. If the soldiers prevented all civilians from moving in and out of the area, the first consequence would be that the target would likely not be able to escape. The second consequence would be that civilians would start to hate American troops for unnecessarily depriving them of their freedom. And they would be, in a way, correct. For the sake of one man, the soldiers were limiting the freedom of many.

That Special Operations Team calculated the risks and decided to be less rigid in their policing: They allowed people to leave the area if they did not match the description of the target. This move, they decided, would not jeopardize the goal of finding the target and would go a long way towards keeping safety and order in the area, since it would quiet much of the civilians' resentment. As it turned out, the civilians who were let through actually provided the soldiers with intelligence, pointing out buildings and correcting them when they focused on the wrong places.

The Army learned the hard way that building relationships with civilians would be important to winning the war. Alex Horton, former infantryman in Iraq, describes what happened when the Army focused exclusively on securing geographic terrain and ignored the battle over the "human terrain" (the people):

> When our platoon entered Iraq's volatile Diyala province in early 2007, children at a school plugged their ears just before an IED exploded beneath one of our vehicles. The kids knew what was coming, but they saw no reason to warn us. Instead, they watched us drive right into the ambush. One of our men died, and in the subsequent crossfire, several insurgents and children were killed. We saw Iraqis cheering and dancing at the blast crater as we left the area hours later.[75]

When the Army released a new counterinsurgency strategy that year, called COIN, the tide started to turn. Nathan Wood,

---

[75] Alex Horton. "In Iraq, I raided insurgents. In Virginia, the police raided me." *Washington Post*, 24 July 2015. https://www.washingtonpost.com/opinions/in-iraq-i-raided-insurgents-in-virginia-the-police-raided-me/2015/07/24/2e114e54-2b02-11e5-bd33-395c05608059_story.html?utm_term=.c99d9b4d98d8

former Captain in the Marines and Harvard Law graduate, writes in his analysis of COIN:

> In stark contrast with the prevailing approach in Iraq up to that point, the manual equated counterinsurgency—or COIN—with "armed social work"... The manual directed commanders to "focus on the population, its needs, and its security" and to conceptualize the conflict not as a contest between two opponents but as "a struggle for the population's support."[76]

The Army realized that its success was dependent on local support. As the COIN field manual states, "Insurgents succeed by maintaining turbulence and highlighting local grievances the COIN effort fails to address. COIN forces succeed by eliminating turbulence and helping the host nation meet the populace's basic needs."[77]

Under COIN, fighting no longer involved the unthinking execution of orders and rules. It demanded thinking hard about the moral implications of one's actions. Nathan writes:

> The benefit of removing an insurgent was to be weighed against the cost of killing or injuring the wrong person and creating a new crop of insurgents by accident. Decision-makers were asked to perform "insurgent math."

---

[76] Nathan Wood. "The Ferguson Consensus is Wrong: What Counterinsurgency in Iraq & Afghanistan Teaches Us About Police Militarization and Community Policing." *Lawfare Research Paper Series* (Vol. 3, No.1), 28 April 2015. https://lawfare.s3-us-west-2.amazonaws.com/staging/Lawfare%20Research%20Paper%20Series%20Vol3No1.pdf

[77] *Counterinsurgency*. FM 3-24. US Army, December 2006. http://usacac.army.mil/cac2/Repository/Materials/COIN-FM3-24.pdf

This nuanced thinking is the essence of "discipline," or the practice of discerning and doing the right thing, at the right time, for the right reasons. "Obedience," in contrast, is about the execution of orders. To train people to be disciplined means developing their capacity to think and morally reason for themselves. To train people to obey entails building their capabilities to meet preset rules and orders.

What does discipline look like? In the Iraq and Afghanistan wars, it meant for us, as Americans, that we had to strive, as much as possible, to demonstrate to civilians that we valued their lives as much as we valued ours, and that we trusted them as much as we wanted them to trust us.

During the Iraq war, U.S. soldiers constantly caught Iraqi civilians breaking the rules that they had established. If they had wanted to, they could have said, "Part of our job is to enforce the law. You broke the law, so that's it." But their job was not to enforce every letter of the law. It was to provide stability to an area, which required building relationships. That meant they couldn't just be enforcement-oriented; they had to consider the civilian perspective too. If soldiers discovered people were on the streets after curfew because they had been heading home from work, they would ask them to plan ahead so they could leave earlier instead of arresting them. Some soldiers deliberately chose not to wear their body armor when walking with Iraqi police chiefs or sheikhs, who did not have body armor. By doing so, those soldiers sent the message: "We trust you, we are comfortable with you." When traveling with the Iraqi police, U.S. soldiers would make sure they put some of their men in Iraqi convoys and some of the Iraqi police in theirs when traveling. In each case, soldiers thought through the implications of their actions and weighed all the competing values at stake. They exercised their discretion instead of limiting themselves to a set of orders.

In fact, at times, the law or rules can conflict with our personal values and sense of what is right. In 1951, United States Marine Corps 2nd Lieutenant Conrad Kronholm (Connie to his buddies) was with his friends on a train between New York and Washington, DC. At one stop, an elderly African-American woman got on the crowded train. Connie immediately got up to offer his seat, which the woman hesitantly, but gratefully, accepted. A few moments later, the train's conductor came by and chastised the woman for sitting in the seat; when Connie offered the explanation, the conductor began to chastise him as well. The conductor ordered Connie to take his seat. Connie refused. Not only did he refuse, but his handful of Marine buddies got up as well and stood in solidarity. The conductor walked sheepishly away, not wanting any trouble.

We can argue that Connie's action didn't demonstrate real discipline; it was just the right thing to do. But remember, it was 1951. Integration had not taken hold in all parts of the country. In fact, Connie and his buddies were breaking the law. Connie didn't give up his seat because of some written rules of etiquette. He just did it because he knew it was the right thing to do, regardless of the consequences.

But these are all high-stakes situations. What about more everyday examples? In the previous chapter, we introduced The Cloverleaf School. One of the school's more unusual practices is its method for disciplining students. Instead of simply "punishing" students for misbehavior by, say, taking away their recess, teachers try to enable students to understand the consequences of their actions. If a student gets angry and hits another person, and the teacher chooses to take him away, the teacher would say, "I'm sorry, but my job is to keep everyone safe, which is why I need to keep you at the end of the table. You can earn your way back by showing us that you are safe."

Cloverleaf's main goal is not to enforce straightforward obedience in order to maintain "classroom discipline," but to encourage empathetic thinking. Teachers actually provide students with a visual social-behavior map to help them consider the implications of their behavior: I did this, this is how it impacted others, and this is how I feel as a result. When a student misbehaves, teachers try to provoke critical thought and reflection, asking, "How does your action affect you and the people around you? What could this mean for your life long-term if you continue this choice?" Their focus is on building students' capacity to do the right thing, not on extracting the right behavior through carrots and sticks.

These scenarios illustrate that discipline transcends rule-following. Is discipline about following "values" then? Not quite. We can also treat values, like rules, as "absolutes." Think of how our court of popular opinion instantaneously passes judgment on the "good" or "bad" deeds of anyone unfortunate enough to enter its chambers. And if we're honest with ourselves, we too pass quick judgments on our friends and neighbors based on our value-systems. We treat our values as unchanging and unerring signposts that place "right" on one side and "wrong" on the other. But maybe what really counts is not whether we hold to certain values over others in an "absolute" manner, but how we think through and apply our values.

Let us take "integrity" as an example. We tell our children to always be honest, yet we don't want them to tell grandma that her cooking is bad or the babysitter that she has bad breath. Like integrity, many other values sound absolute, but in reality are situationally dependent. We may say loyalty is an absolute value, yet we shouldn't be loyal to the wrong thing. We say that respect is an absolute value, but if you ask an adolescent from the city what respect is and how you earn it, he will likely give you a different answer than an adolescent from the country.

"Customer-centric" may be a great value, but what if the customer's desires adversely affect the company? Values bend and shift depending on the context.

Here is another combat dilemma that illustrates the situational context of values.

You are a 23-year-old platoon leader ascending a mountain in Afghanistan during winter. Your pack is heavy because, in addition to your usual gear and weapons, you are carrying food, water, medical supplies, and ammunition to last you for three days. Resupply at altitude is difficult, so you and your team are likely on your own. One day into your mission, you reach your first target. The enemy has been decimated by air and artillery strikes. Most, but not all, are already dead. You count four combatants who are still alive, two of whom appear to be teenagers. The Law of Land Warfare clearly states that you must treat and care for the wounded, even if they are on the opposing side.[78] Though you quickly discern that no amount of medical attention is likely to keep them alive for more than a few hours, you must make a decision. Do you use your limited medical supplies on the wounded enemy soldiers, or do you keep them because they may be required to save one of your own soldiers at some point in the next two days? What is the right thing to do?

Think about the soldier in the scenario above. How does he apply the Army values in this incident? Loyalty: Does he show loyalty to the law, to his fellow soldiers, or to the mission? Duty: Does duty bind him to the mission or to the enemy's treatment? Personal Courage: Is it courageous to help these wounded men and risk his men's lives, or to disobey the law?

---

[78] *The Law of Land Warfare*. FM 27-10. US Army, July 1956. http://www.aschq.army.mil/gc/files/fm27-10.pdf

And finally, Integrity: Does he do what he feels is right based on what the law or his conscience says?

The point here is that we have to prepare and train people, like that soldier, to think through how to apply their values. While many approach ethics and compliance as a matter of obedience to set rules, what we really need is discipline, which is doing the right thing, at the right time, for the right reasons, regardless of the consequences.

The capacity to discern and do the right thing is necessary in an ambiguous and complex reality, where there are no strict black-and-white rules to apply. Take the example of Levi Strauss, an apparel company. Thomas Donaldson, a Wharton Business School professor, narrates its story in a *Harvard Business Review* article.

> It [Levi Strauss] discovered in the early 1990s that two of its suppliers in Bangladesh were employing children under the age of 14—a practice that violated the company's principles, but was tolerated in Bangladesh. Forcing the suppliers to fire the children would not have ensured that the children received an education, and it would have caused serious hardship for the families depending on the children's wages.[79]

Simply applying the rules or even consulting Levi Strauss' corporate values would probably have provided little satisfactory help. In order to discern the right thing to do, the company's leaders had to critically think through all the facets of the situation in line with the company's values.

---

[79] Thomas Donaldson. "Values in Tension: Ethics Away from Home." *Harvard Business Review*, September-October 1996. https://hbr.org/1996/09/values-in-tension-ethics-away-from-home

Here is how Levi resolved it:

> In a creative arrangement, the suppliers agreed to pay the children's regular wages while they attended school and to offer each child a job at age 14. Levi, in turn, agreed to pay the children's tuition and provide books and uniforms. That arrangement allowed Levi to uphold its principles and provide long-term benefits to its host country.

This type of creative and critical thinking is not how we tend to "do" ethics and compliance in our organizations. Usually, the organizations' leaders devise a set of values that undergird a systematized set of standards, rules and policies on behavior. The leaders might even assess their people's behavior against these standards in performance reviews. Organizations have scaled systems of training, development, and accountability, leaving little space for human discretion. Because decisions do not occur in a vacuum, what organizations need to develop is not moral obedience, but moral thinking and discipline—wrestling with and applying the right values in order to do the right thing. It is not, after all, a straight line from your organization's values to the right decision.

So far, we have argued that it is important to equip people to do the right thing, instead of enforcing obedience to pre-determined "right" answers. But let us say that you develop and trust people to do the right thing, but someone makes a major mistake and does, even by her or his own admission, the wrong thing. How should you respond?

Responding to Failure

John Wood, whom we introduced earlier in Chapter One and Two, was a fairly high performer in the Army. He was promoted, given extra responsibility, and admired by his peers. Then, while deployed in Iraq, he made a huge mistake: He broke, in his own words, one of the "cardinal rules" of the military profession.[80] This misstep was so serious that he was forced to transfer to another platoon that played more of a "support" role. John had a month to wait for his transfer to happen. During this month, he had a lot of time to think about what he did.

"I replayed the whole moment over and over again in my head. There was a period where I wanted to walk outside and hopefully just get shot because that would wash away all my sins and I would die honorably," he said.

But in the process of John's re-assignment, Sergeant Robert Adams intervened. He told John that he had seen him in action before, and that, if he was willing, he could join his platoon, the first platoon of the Charlie Company. They talked for over three hours.

"Robert was the first guy who ever asked me, 'What did you learn from that?' He told me, 'Whatever happened in the past is in the past. I want you to be the best version of you that you can be. Put all that stuff in the past and help these guys out.' I got another opportunity to either succeed or fail," John said. He is now a fitness instructor at Fort Jackson.

To be clear, John did not feel that he had to be good because he felt indebted to Robert. What Robert did was help him recognize the good already inside of him, which then inspired

---

[80] It is not important in this example to specify John's mistake. What is important is that his mistake was not intentional or malicious in nature, nor a violation of Army values, but it was still viewed across the organization as a major mistake. Even though John made this mistake as a junior soldier, he still felt that it would have been just as bad if a more seasoned soldier had done it.

him to try again. John said, "He inspired me to be the best version of myself that I could be, even though I fucked up."

Robert's platoon was consistently chosen to take on some of the Army's toughest and most important missions. But it was also unique in that Robert had taken on three men, including John, who were "rehabilitative transfers": Soldiers who got into trouble and were moved into a new unit to give them a fresh start. "It would not be inaccurate to say that some people would have seen Robert's platoon as a dumping ground," John said. They were deemed "screw-ups" who were not bright, fit, motivated or disciplined enough.

But Robert, a multiple-time combat veteran, did not care about his men's past failures. He wanted everyone to take initiative, to think three or five steps past the plan. It was the first time, John said, that he was in a culture where even the littlest guy had a say. Robert was not just concerned about the success of the mission, but about the development of the men under him and how they could succeed after they left his platoon.

While in Sergeant Adams' platoon, John was in charge of a group of guys who were generally dismissed for not being "good enough." For the first month, they were fairly apathetic, doing what they were told in a slow, uninspired manner. John decided to do to them what Robert did to him: Get to know them, believe in them, and give them a second chance.

"In the Army, anyone who is not a stud right out of the gate gets overlooked and becomes invisible. I saw all these good qualities in them and tried to make them better, which in the process made me better. All I really did was to get to know them. I talked to them when nobody else wanted to do so. When people screwed up, you have to be the person that says, 'Yeah, you screwed up, but what did you learn from that?' It's not about the mistake; it's how you move forward from that mistake that defines you," he said.

After a few months, his team ramped up its effort and energy. They were even assigned to be the main squad for a high-value target raid, a responsibility usually reserved for teams that rank one level higher.

Reflecting on the difficulty of moving forward, John said, "The hardest part was forgiving myself. This is true for a lot of people who perform highly until they make a mistake. But you have to be in an environment that kind of allows that, because I didn't really forgive myself until I started working for Adams."

Too often, leaders believe it is part of their job to continually point out mistakes and shortcomings, to hold their people against lofty standards, all in order to "inspire" people to get better. But frequent criticism often leads to shame, and shame "corrodes the very part of us that believes we can change and do better," according to Brené Brown, a research professor.[81] When people screw up, as John's story illustrates, they need a re-affirmation of their potential, one that does not dilute the standards to which you hold them. This means helping them reflect on the past to learn lessons for the future and offering them a second chance.

Essentially, building capacity in others means affirming their potential. Think about it: *To develop capability is to uphold standards over people; to develop capacity, then, is to uphold people over standards*. In a capacity-centered approach, when people do something wrong, you believe that they are far more

---

[81] Brené Brown. *Daring Greatly: How the courage to be vulnerable transforms the way we live, love, parent, and lead*. New York: Gotham Books, 2012, p. 72.

than their transgressions. You help them see that there is more goodness to them than they see in themselves.

Guiding Principles

How do we cultivate internal discipline, and not just external obedience? Here are a few principles that can guide us onto the right track:

1. Emotional intelligence and empathy are essential. We are not arguing for situational ethics, but rather for using emotional intelligence to understand the secondary and tertiary effects of one's actions. Although empathy can be considered a "touchy feely" concept, its importance cannot be overstated. If the soldier in our previous scenario chooses to obey the law and treat the wounded enemy, he must be able to think through the impact of his decision on his soldiers for the rest of the trip. He must use his emotional intelligence and his empathy.

2. If your outcome is about you, you are probably wrong. If your outcome is ultimately self-serving, odds are that you are not applying values correctly. Conversely, if you are thinking of others or something larger than yourself, you are on the path to applying your values correctly. Recall the definition of discipline: doing the right thing, at the right time, for the right reasons, regardless of the consequences.

3. Actions versus habits. Making a mistake when trying to apply one's values is radically different from lacking values. The former is usually confined to a single act, but the latter manifests in repeated actions or habits. Let us say that a general is caught in an adulterous relationship. Is his action indicative of a lack of scruples

throughout his career (and it is only now that he is caught), or is his choice mostly confined to the situation and not a reflection of who he is as a man? What about a journalist that exaggerates a story? Has everything she reported lacked integrity, or did she get wrapped up in a hubristic moment? We tend to brand individuals like these with a scarlet letter, but we must look beyond individual acts and examine repeated decisions.

4. Individuals are more important than organizations. Though this is a provocative statement, consider that some of the best organizations in the world practice this principle. If you apply values for the good of the people in your organization, your organization will be better off. The moment you put your organization above your people, you begin to apply values as absolutes, and your people will start to leave for an organization that values them more. Think of the backlash that the CEO of AOL received in 2014 when he cited two "distressed babies" that cost AOL "a million dollars each" as examples of cost pressures that led the company to cut back employee health benefits. If we take his words at face value, he was presumably thinking of the good of the organization as a whole, while neglecting the impact of his words on a few individuals.[82] Humans are messy and complicated; they require a nuanced and flexible treatment that rules cannot provide. In fact, organizations alone can adhere to absolute values and rules, because they consist of abstractions (e.g. legal structures, balance sheets, org charts) — they are not living and breathing individuals.

---

[82] There are many additional layers to this situation. For more information, see an interview with one of the mothers of those babies. Kristen Bellstrom. "This mother, who was shamed by a CEO, says women and children are 'easy targets.'" *Fortune*, 18 July 2015. http://fortune.com/2015/07/18/deanna-fei-book-aol/

Figuring out the right thing to do is a complex matter that requires much more than the straightforward application of values. Sometimes the right thing to do in one situation is not the right thing in another. Sometimes doing what you deem to be right will look like the wrong thing according to the rulebook. It is a lot easier to be blindly obedient than to cultivate and practice discipline.

A Values-Application Metaphor

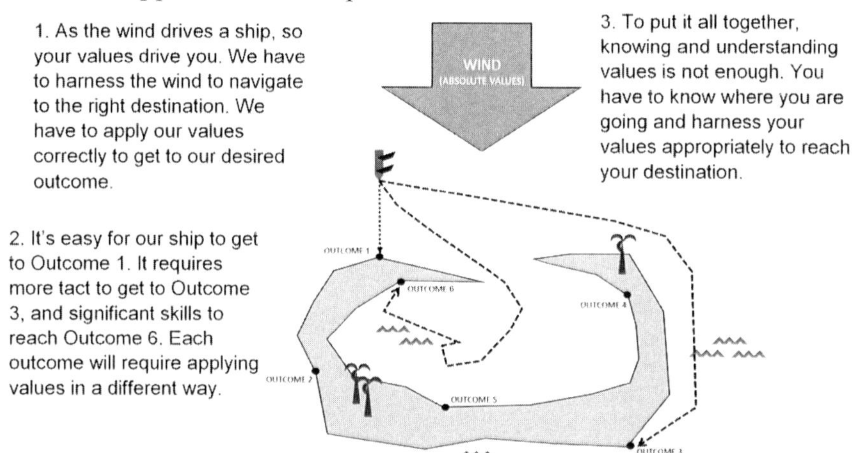

As Ralph Waldo Emerson once wrote in *Self-Reliance*, "The voyage of the best ship is a zigzag line of a hundred tacks. See the line from a sufficient distance, and it straightens itself to the average tendency. Genuine action will explain itself, and will explain other genuine actions."

Amatoris adjutus, Advocati animatos
(Amateurs Motivate, Professionals Inspire)

Chapter 6 | Capacity Building: Culture & Leadership

Let's say that you apply everything that we have written so far in this book and redesign a certain program or set of processes in your organization. The truth is that you may very well still fail.

Leadership and culture matter more than any specific program or process. If you launch a "capacity-building" program tomorrow, no matter how great it turns out to be, a bad culture will inevitably stifle the impact of the program. If your boss approves your enrollment in an awesome "leadership development" course, but constantly micromanages and fixates on every mistake you make, then there is no room for the lessons from the course to take root.

If we analogize "capacity" to a green plant, then an organization's leadership and culture are equivalent to soil, without which plants eventually wither. A great capacity-building training program may produce some short-term results, but these results will not be sustained or integrated into the fabric of the organization.

This final chapter will explore the kind of leadership and organizational culture that enables capacity-building processes to flourish. Building capacity is not just a matter of taking best practices from this book or elsewhere and inserting them into your programs. It requires a whole new way of relating to and leading others.

Culture

It was a snowy winter in Afghanistan. A group of Rangers was sent to capture a high-value target, who was determined to be within a large compound that contained several houses. Sixteen Rangers were sent to secure all the women and children and consolidate them into one room. Highly senior officials were monitoring this mission, so the Rangers' leaders were counting the minutes until the men finished their assignment.

The time was ticking, but the Rangers still hadn't returned. Perplexed by how long they were taking, the leaders suddenly saw all sixteen Rangers walking towards them, carrying women and children on their backs. Some of them were carrying three kids, one on each arm and another on their backs. Others were carrying a woman on their backs and a kid in front.

"There's snow on the ground, and they have no shoes," the Rangers explained. Their leaders immediately nodded and understood. If they had chosen to trudge the women and children through the snow, they would not have violated any rules. But they appropriately applied the Army's values and chose to do the right thing.

They did what they did not because of a plan, strategy, manual, mission or vision statement. They did the right thing because it was part of their culture.

If an organization's mission and vision provide "what" an organization aims to do and "how" it tries to accomplish this, then culture provides the "who." In the 1940s, businesses began to develop mission statements, most likely due to an influx of veterans—who were accustomed to following Army missions—in the workforce. Vision statements started to appear shortly thereafter in the 1950's.[83] Both had a tremendous impact on business: mission statements told organizations what they did, and vision statements told them where they were going and how to get there.

Neither of these documents, however, addresses the discipline of the leaders and employees. Organizations want and need their people to do the right thing, at the right time, for the right reason. They want their people to internalize this discipline so they can act, not re-act, in unpredictable circumstances. The sixteen Rangers quickly made that decision to help carry the women and children without consulting a manual or their supervisors—they didn't have time to do so, in any case. But they knew that doing so was the right thing to do, and that part of what it meant to be a Ranger was to do the right thing.

You can think of an organization's culture as an internalized system of guidance—a set of norms (explicit or implicit) that

---

[83] If we search through Google Books' Ngram viewer, an online search engine for phrases in books, the phrase "mission statement" starts appearing in the early 1940s. "Vision statement" appears a little later, in the mid-1950s.

informs how people lead, make decisions, communicate and generally behave. Doing the right thing is, of course, a key value of the Rangers, but it was ultimately the Rangers' culture that created space for people to apply this value in their own way. Culture cannot be boiled down to a static list of values. Rather, it comes alive as people wrestle with their values in different situations. As we said before in Chapter Five, a common value like "respect" can have radically different meanings depending on the context.

What does an ideal culture look like? Let's recognize upfront that all organizations do have cultures. Few, however, try to deliberately shape theirs. Each organization should develop its own culture in its own way and answer for itself what an ideal culture looks like.

But if an organization's culture is going to prioritize capacity over capability, then one thing needs to be true: People must be valued above all else. An organization's values or culture statement could be very thoughtfully crafted and well-designed. But people are unlikely to care about "living out" those values unless they believe that their organization values them not just for what they can do for the organization, but for who they are.

National Football League (NFL)

The NFL has received intense public scrutiny for some football players' violent behaviors in their homes. Realizing that it will face responsibility for these players' private actions, the NFL has mandated that all its players undergo training on domestic violence, child abuse, and sexual assault.[84] While its

---

[84] Lindsay H. Jones. "NFL begins new phase of domestic violence education as training camps open." *USA Today*, 27 July 2015. http://www.usatoday.com/story/sports/nfl/2015/07/27/domestic-violence-training-education-drunk-driving-intervention/30752175/

intentions are laudable, this initiative runs counter to the main message the league communicates to its players.

The NFL's treatment of players is predicated upon the separation of the "professional" from the "human." Players are evaluated, traded, and moved in accordance with their abilities and what they do for teams; they are seen as valuable pieces of meat. Coaches confine their responsibility to players' behavior on the field, partly because of the nature of the NFL's rules. For instance, according to the league's rules, a coach cannot give players financial advice. This separation is wise in some circumstances, but it can preclude opportunities for coaches to support players. Imagine a new player telling his coach that he wants to buy a house. The coach might think to himself, "I hope he is going to pay cash for that and not sign up for a 30-year mortgage because he might not be working in four years," but he can't legally say anything.

When Chris Ballard, director of player personnel for the Kansas City Chiefs, took the stage at the NFL Rookie Symposium in 2013, he said, "Most of you will not be in this league three years from now... Nobody cares about your problems. The fans don't care. The media doesn't care. And ownership doesn't care. They care about results."[85] Afterwards, Jimmy Stewart, a former defensive back and licensed therapist who works with athletes and veterans, commented, "He was treating them exactly how they feel, like objects."

Knowing that they could be traded next year without notice, players learn to look out for their own interests and to feel no genuine loyalty to their teams. They do not really care if their

---

[85] Alyssa Roenigk. "Lotus Pose on Two." *ESPN*, 21 August 2013. http://www.espn.com/nfl/story/_/id/9581925/seattle-seahawks-use-unusual-techniques-practice-espn-magazine

behavior reflects poorly upon their team or the NFL at large. They know the NFL is only interested in how their personal behaviors affect the league's reputation. To most of them, the NFL does not have much authority to tell them what to do in their personal lives.

Players are free agents, accountable only to themselves and their reputations. Many players show up on time to practices because they will be fined for not doing so, not because they are concerned about the impact of their tardiness on their teams. Adding rules or sanctions can worsen the problem, as these measures treat players like animals that need to be corralled. Telling players the team's values is slightly better, but it begs the question, "Why should I care about this team enough that I want to live out its values and represent it in public? Why should I care about doing right by my team?" Inspiring the discipline of doing the right thing for one's team is near impossible in a culture that does not care about people.

Before trying to change behavior, it is important to first ask, "Why?" Why does this player always show up late to practice? Why does this player beat his wife? Why should this player care about this team enough to want to embody its values? Effective behavioral-change begins from a posture of understanding.[86] Despite the culture of the league as a whole, individual teams can still stand out in how they treat their players. The Seattle Seahawks are a good example. After winning the NFC Championship game and beating the San Francisco 49ers in 2014, Richard Sherman, the Seattle Seahawks' cornerback, caused a stir when he called the 49ers' Michael Crabtree a "sorry" wide receiver in a FOX Sports interview.

---

[86] It is extremely important to state that players misbehave for reasons that are not justified or even simple. The reasons why people commit domestic violence, child abuse or sexual assault, for instance, are complex, and may involve both historical and individual factors. See article in the above footnote for more details.

That day, his coach, Pete Carroll, took him aside to chat. Coach Carroll said that he approached the conversation like a father with his son. He wanted Sherman to realize that he "caused a stir that took something away from the team."[87] (A year later, when chances were high that Richard's son would be born on Super Bowl Sunday, there was a lot of speculation as to whether Richard would sit out the game. Pete unsurprisingly said, "It's about family first and we will support his decision.")[88]

Shortly after, Richard publicly apologized for attacking an individual and taking attention away from his team's victory. He also published an article entitled, "A Love Letter to Coach Carroll," even though his coach had called him out.[89] Richard's loyalty to his team and coach enabled him to understand that he was not an independent actor: His actions, even off the field, could hurt or help his team. Indeed, in an op-ed in which Sherman explained his biting remarks, he also called out Seahawks fans for throwing food at 49ers' linebacker Navorro Bowman as he was carted off for an injury. He told them that they were better than that and that players deserved better than that.[90]

The culture of the Seahawks is not accidental, but

---

[87]"Carroll has father-son talk with Sherman about angry remarks." *St Louis Post-Dispatch*, 21 January 2014. http://www.stltoday.com/sports/football/carroll-has-father-son-talk-with-sherman-about-angry-remarks/article_a1c65ce7-94db-5e92-bea0-1e5be3987708.html

[88] Jared Dubin. "Super Bowl 49: Carroll: 'Family First' when It comes to Sherman's son's birth." *CBS Sports*, 30 January 2015. http://www.cbssports.com/nfl/story/25009589/carroll-family-first-when-it-comes-to-shermans-sons-birth

[89] Richard Sherman. "A Love Letter to Coach Carroll." *MMQB*, 31 January 2014. http://mmqb.si.com/2014/01/31/super-bowl-48-richard-sherman-pete-carroll

[90] Richard Sherman. "To Those Who Would Call Me a Thug or Worse ..." *MMQB*, 20 January 2014. http://mmqb.si.com/2014/01/20/richard-sherman-interview-michael-crabtree

intentionally shaped by Coach Carroll's leadership and philosophy. Michael Silver, sportswriter and television analyst for the NFL network, once asked Coach Carroll, "A lot of coaches are obsessed with controlling players and getting them to behave a certain way on and off the field. You seem to have a real different philosophy. What's your view on that?"[91]

Coach Carroll responded, "I'm obsessed in a different way. We really try and help our players be the best that they can be. We want to create an environment where they do things because they want to not because they have to. We are not forcing them or coercing them." This sounds remarkably like our discussion of internalized discipline: doing the right thing, at the right time, for the right reason, regardless of the consequences.

Richard's description of his coach's philosophy echoes Sergeant Robert Adams' leadership style, discussed in Chapter Five: "He finds the positives when we lose, in addition to the things we can improve on. I've never been on a team where the coaching staff was so positive. There isn't a lot of yelling and cursing at players. There's no talking down to players. It's about conversations, not aggression."[92]

How did Coach Carroll, who is lauded for taking the Seahawks to their first Super Bowl victory in 2014, develop this approach for coaching NFL players? The origins of his ethos date back to his days coaching University of Southern California (USC)'s football team.

"It hit me that in our days at USC, many of our players were drafted high, but a lot of them didn't do very well in the league,"

---

[91] *Carroll's philosophy*. NFL. www.nfl.com/videos/nfl-network-gameday/0ap2000000320158/Carroll-s-philosophy

[92] Richard Sherman. "A Love Letter to Coach Carroll." *MMQB*, 31 January 2014. http://mmqb.si.com/2014/01/31/super-bowl-48-richard-sherman-pete-carroll

Coach Carroll said. "They would come back to visit campus and say: 'It's hard-core. You don't know anybody. You go home and you're by yourself. You don't feel connected at all.' We had reached guys at a different level that allowed them to perform at a high level. And when they left us, they didn't have the support to carry them through."[93]

He began to reimagine the culture of an NFL team. "I wanted to find out if we went to the NFL and really took care of guys, really cared about each and every individual, what would happen?" he said.

He is known for his "Win Forever" philosophy. To him, winning is not just about getting the right numbers on the board. "Of course we want to win every game, but winning forever is more about realizing your potential and making yourself as good as you can be," he said. "Realizing that is a tremendous accomplishment, whether it's in football or in life."[94]

His first and foremost goal is to help each player realize his potential, or, in other words, develop his capacity. It is no wonder that Dr. Michael Gervais, a sports psychologist who works closely with him, described Coach Carroll's coaching philosophy as "athlete first, execution second."[95] In other words: Person over performance.

---

[93] Alyssa Roenigk. "Lotus Pose on Two." *ESPN*, 21 August 2013. http://espn.go.com/nfl/story/_/id/9581925/seattle-seahawks-use-unusual-techniques-practice-espn-magazine

[94] "The Essence of Pete Carroll's 'Win Forever' Philosophy." *Seahawks*, 10 January 2014. http://www.seahawks.com/news/2014/01/29/essence-pete-carrolls-win-forever-philosophy

[95] Michael Schottey. "Pete Carrol Shares the Seahawks' Winning Philosophy with Bleacher Report." *Bleacher Report*, 11 January 2013. http://bleacherreport.com/articles/1480332-pete-carroll-shares-the-seahawks-winning-philosophy-with-bleacher-report

Leadership

Leaders have many responsibilities. They have to ensure that the organization's goals are met, strategies are devised, and tasks are successfully executed. These *managerial* responsibilities are important, but they cannot override the *leadership* responsibility to develop and care for people. It is really this simple: Managers care about procedures, processes, and accountability. Leaders care about people.

Mind you, we didn't write, "Leaders care about people's capacity." As this chapter makes clear, we are talking about valuing people holistically – for both their professional abilities and personal needs.

These days, it is popular for leaders to talk about how much they value their people. It's easy to value people, but it's much harder to do so when there is an apparent trade-off involved. This is not unique to the military, sports, and business; it also occurs in education. Most teachers are absolutely and sincerely wedded to their student's success. But, much like the NFL rules, the rules and pressures in education can make teachers care less about individual students and more about meeting the standards of their organizations.

Leaders, whether in the battlefield, boardroom or classroom, say that they value people. But they tend to only do so when it doesn't conflict with the success and goals of the organization, strategy or task—when it doesn't conflict with their managerial responsibilities. We will examine each one of these three supposed trade-offs.

Leadership Lesson #1: People > Organization

Some leaders may be reading this and thinking, "We get it: People matter. But we have limited resources, so the organization's needs have to come first." This mindset elevates leaders' (managerial) responsibility to the organization's budget over their (leadership) care for people's needs.

To highlight the shortcomings of this mindset, let's take a look at the Ranger Regiment, an elite special operation force within the Army that predates the Revolutionary War. It conducts missions ranging from hostage rescue to high-value target captures. The Rangers hold themselves to higher standards – physical and otherwise – than most soldiers; their ringing motto is: "Rangers lead the way!"[96]

People tend to attribute the Ranger Regiment's success to the fact that it gets the best talent.[97] What really distinguishes the Regiment from other units, however, is its loyalty to its warriors and their families.

The Regiment takes care of its people, and the people take care of the mission. If a Ranger's child is sick, the child can go straight to the Ranger doctor, instead of having to go through a regular hospital. This holds true even if the Ranger leaves the Regiment for another unit. The Rangers are motivated to push themselves as hard as possible for the mission partly because they trust the Regiment to take care of them; they do not need to worry too much about their own needs. Their capacity to give increases.

---

[96] Part of the Ranger creed states: "Acknowledging the fact that a Ranger is a more elite soldier, who arrives at the cutting edge of battle by land, sea, or air, I accept the fact that as a Ranger, my country expects me to move further, faster, and fight harder than any other soldier." The Ranger Physical Fitness test, administered to students on the first day of Ranger School, is 60 push-ups, 70 sit-ups, 10 chin-ups, and 5 miles in 37 minutes. Ranger School is a requirement for all leaders in the Ranger Regiment.

[97] Former General Stanley McChrystal framed it more accurately: It wasn't that Special Operations got the "best" people, but that it got the "best available" people – a fact both humbling and inspiring.

In contrast, when employees sense that their organization cares only about taking as much as it can from them, they start to zero in on protecting their needs. Take Abigail, a friend who used to work at a local city agency in New York.

Abigail's manager ruled that every minute that she is late to work has to be deducted from her salary, which is set at an hourly rate. If she was tardy due to subway delays, she had to obtain proof from the public transportation system that the subway she took was indeed delayed and submit a claim to HR. She said, "If I am late to work by a few minutes, I am the kind of person who would make it up by cutting my lunch break short by a few minutes. But since my manager was invested in taking every penny from me, I feel motivated to take a full 60-minute lunch break and leave right at 5pm and not a minute later."

When both parties try to get as much as they can for themselves, then the employer-employee relationship is defined by mistrust and calculation, instead of loyalty and generosity. Few things can damage trust more than feeling like your manager is mainly interested in taking as much as possible from you, and supporting you only insofar as it fulfills her or his goals. Just see what happened to Jay Ramsay.

Jay, a company controller, got a phone call one day informing him that the doctors were arranging for an emergency delivery for his pregnant wife because the baby had stopped moving.[98] The delivery was successful and Jay took off the rest of the week. When he returned to work, his boss scolded him in

---

[98] Josh Levs. "Stop Punishing the Family Man." *Harvard Business Review*, May 2015. https://hbr.org/2015/05/stop-punishing-the-family-man?utm_source=Socialflow&utm_medium=Tweet&utm_campaign=Socialflow

a private meeting for taking off work as he "should have known and planned better." Since he had a standing job offer elsewhere, he quit his job at the end of the meeting. Josh Levs, who tells this story about Jay in a *Harvard Business Review* article, writes that Jay feels that his new employer not only respects him as an employee, he respects him as a father. And in return, his bosses have in him "an employee who is absolutely dedicated." (As an aside, Jay's former colleagues told him his eventual replacement turned out to be 'a nightmare.')

All these examples demonstrate that valuing people means more than just valuing their capacity to contribute. It also means valuing their personal, financial and material needs. It is not enough simply to have a "lofty purpose" and expect people to give their all towards it.

Of course, an organization that does nothing but meet the needs of its members will not effectively accomplish its shared goals. But the leader's role is to make the organization's and individual's goals and needs converge as much as possible. Years ago, when the Army decided that it needed to provide its officer corps with growth opportunities, it developed partnerships with the FBI, Federal Trade Commission, corporations, state departments, and other organizations that agreed to give Army soldiers short-term internships. This arrangement obviously benefits soldiers, as it gives them excellent, civilian experience to put on their resume for when they leave the Army. But it also benefits the Army by facilitating relationships with key organizations. The Army, naturally, takes the chance that a soldier might leave the Army and commit full-time to one of his or her assigned organizations. You might think, "All that investment only for the soldier to leave?" But the Army benefits from having its people in strategic places. Many consulting firms cultivate a strong alumni network for just this reason.

Unless an organization is willing to invest in people's needs even if they conflict with the organizations in the short-run, it will have a hard time holding onto its people.[99] What makes the Rangers special is really quite simple. Their leaders understand that it is not enough to attract the best talent. They have to deeply value the personal needs and developmental goals of their men if they are to retain the best talent.

Leadership Lesson #2: People > Strategy

Some readers may be thinking, "I get that people can come up with their own answers, but leaders should determine an organization's strategy or direction. That strategy should override what people want to do." In this framework, leaders' (managerial) responsibility to the organization's strategy overrides their (leadership) responsibility to developing their people's capacity to contribute. There is some wisdom to this, but let's return to The Cloverleaf School, which we introduced in Chapter Four, to illustrate the limitations of this mindset.

It's common sense that teachers are the experts, and students ought to learn from them. Teachers ought then to set the curriculum direction (or "strategy") for the classroom. But The Cloverleaf School takes a slightly different approach. Emily Swindall, Educational Director, emphasizes that teachers and students co-create the learning experience. "Teachers bring the knowledge of supposed-to. They know the standards, and kids know what they are interested in," she said.

---

[99] According to a study by the Society for Human Resource Management, it costs organizations the equivalent of six to nine months of an employee's salary to hire and train a replacement. Julie Kantor. "High Turnover Costs Way More Than You Think." *Huffington Post*, 11 February 2016. http://www.huffingtonpost.com/julie-kantor/high-turnover-costs-way-more-than-you-think_b_9197238.html

"At the beginning of the unit, we co-create goals. So as a teacher I might say, 'Hey guys, we are going to work on our commas.' Another kid might say, 'I'm really interested in robots.' So I'll say, 'That's awesome. Let's make those two work together.' It's a delicate balance," she explained. A student was into robots, so he built a robot for his culminating project and wrote an explanation of it with proper usage of commas. Another student was into yoga, so he taught his class a yoga sequence when they were learning about Asia. As students learn and explore, they often develop new interests and are encouraged to pursue them at Cloverleaf.

While leaders can certainly provide a strategy or game-plan, they need to create space for others to not just contribute, but to rethink their ideas. People will only feel like they are genuinely co-creating when nothing is sacred, when everything – vision, goals, means, and values – is up for discussion and revision.[100]

To co-create a strategy or a solution is much deeper than to simply "work together" or to "collaborate." Co-creation is shared ownership over outcomes, grounded in deep understanding of one another.[101] When the opposite is true, when people are commanded to do something without any room for input, they feel disrespected.

According to Peter Moskos, a former Baltimore officer, he and his fellow officers did not react well when their district's commanding officer issued an informal quota of two arrests a

---

[100] In previous chapters, we've discussed how capacity-building is about giving people the outcome and letting them figure out how to get there. Now we are pushing our argument further by saying that inspirational leaders encourage people, as much as is possible, to shape strategic goals and outcomes.

[101] Co-creation without co-recognition is a halfway job. If someone is actively co-creating something with you, then that person deserves to share credit and recognition—if not, ownership will always be partial and never complete, because the stakes will be lower for the unrecognized team member.

month and demanded that those who failed to meet it submit written justification.[102] Officers resented being told what to do. Even officers who were previously aggressive in their enforcement reduced their arrests. "Total arrests [went] down as we felt anything even looking like a quota was an insult to our professionalism," Peter, now a professor at the John Jay College of Criminal Justice, said in an email interview.

The officers' behavior makes sense in the context of a larger study conducted of over 20,000 employees around world.[103] The leadership behavior that had the biggest impact on employees – more than providing recognition or communicating an inspiring vision – was treating others with respect. To micromanage adults and issue preemptory orders without explanation is to treat adults like children; it is inherently disrespectful. People need to feel a sense of agency in their work.

Some may say, "But doesn't co-creation create a chaotic environment? What holds a team together if we remove deference to higher authority?" It is important to share a common vision and set of values, but the most important glue is "deep understanding" of one another. Deep understanding requires suspending one's reality in order to step into another's mindset, priorities and values. It requires understanding what others care about, what activates them and where they draw their lines.

Unfortunately, people are usually not trained to understand others. Instead, they believe that they need to "win friends and influence people." This mindset becomes a game of convincing

[102] Peter Moskos. *A Cop in the Hood: My Year Policing Baltimore's Eastern District.* Princeton: Princeton University Press, 2009, pp. 152-155.
[103] Christine Porath. "Half of Employees Don't Feel Respected by Their Bosses." *Harvard Business Review*, 29 November 2014. https://hbr.org/2014/11/half-of-employees-dont-feel-respected-by-their-bosses

another person to give up her or his framework and enter into your way of seeing the world. This is how we recruit customers, clients, voters, talent, and so on. They are "problems" that must be solved or "objects" of manipulation, not people to be understood.[104]

What are meaningful ways to enable shared understanding (beyond happy-hour socials)? First, shared experience is a key way to accelerate shared understanding. In football for instance, defensive lines, who are responsible for rushing the quarterback and defeating the offensive scheme, can sometimes get frustrated. They may see the kicker as some guy who just stands around and kicks some balls while they are sweating their hearts out in practice and in games. Yet the kicker and the linesmen are on the same team with the same mission and goals.

What they are missing is a shared understanding and appreciation of each other's roles and talents. What if the kicker participated in some of the defensive line's workouts, and the defensive linesmen tried to kick a 30-yard field goal? Both sides would learn more about each other and, in turn, appreciate each other more. Perhaps the defensive line might learn that the kicker used to be a quarterback in high school and has a natural leadership ability to rally the team together in high-pressure situations. Or they may learn that he was heavily recruited as a soccer player and turned down significant contracts due to his love of the game of football. Once we focus on enabling deeper understanding of one another, the possibilities are endless.

Second, nothing inspires collaboration in a team more than realizing that each teammate is dependent on the other—a sense of interdependency. The Army, more than most organizations,

---

[104] There is some great work by Barry Jentz, in his book *Talking Sense* that explains in more detail how leaders can do this.

understands the truism: You are only as strong as your weakest link.

Aaron Welch, introduced earlier in Chapter Two, was a sniper squad leader who led a platoon on ten-day-long reconnaissance missions to gather intelligence on the enemy. Strategizing for a reconnaissance mission requires a lot of time and careful thought. You need to thoughtfully plan your routes, identifying infiltration routes, exfiltration routes, alternate routes, and so on. You have to be careful not to double back because if you go back to the same places twice you stand a better chance of being captured or killed.

Aaron had a lot of young men in his platoon who were smart, but not quite "performance-ready." While most leaders would have let the experienced guys determine the strategy, he decided to rotate ownership over route-planning, letting even junior sergeants take charge of the routes. After someone had planned a route strategy, he would tell the next person how he did it and what he learned from it. By distributing responsibility and ensuring that everyone was learning from one another, Aaron's platoon cut the planning time by more than half, from a few days to twelve hours. But it was not always pretty.

"Sometimes people failed. We wouldn't say, 'You're fired because of that one time.' We said, 'OK that was bad,' and we would allow them to learn from it and get another chance to prove themselves," he said.

"Even though our lives were at stake, it was the only way to get better," Aaron explained. "We were one of the more successful groups in the region because we let people learn through trial and error. And for these young sergeants who were planning the routes – remember, their lives were at stake too."

As you can see, developing people may come at the expense of the successful execution of tasks. It is not always an obvious win-win. Aaron's platoon had to embrace the risk of failure, even if it meant putting lives at risk. But it was worth it, for that was the only way to develop his entire team's capacity to learn, grow, and succeed in the long run. Building collective team capacity was critical because no one was fully indispensable. "If someone got injured or went on vacation, someone else knew how to do his job. Our team was stronger because everybody knew how to do everything," he said.

There are ways to cultivate that sense of interdependency in settings other than war, and it can happen in places where we least expect it.

Corbett, a seven-year-old football player, was a talented young man who always paid attention to what was going on around him. One late fall evening, he noticed that one of his teammates was struggling to keep up with a run at the end of a long practice. Corbett had already finished his run, but as soon as he crossed the finish line, he turned around right in front of the coaches and started running against the flow of human traffic. The coaches were yelling at him to come back, asking him what he was doing. His teammates passed him going the other way with quizzical looks. He reached the last boy in the run, turned around and started running back with that teammate to inspire him to finish and keep going. One by one, his teammates joined him. The coaches stood silent.[105]

That day, a new team habit was born. Every practice, as soon as a boy was finished with his exercises, he went back to

[105] Some might say that Corbett was a special kid or that this was a special circumstance. Neither is probably true. Many times our younger generations "get it" intuitively, and an older generation either doubts their capacity or steers them toward an old solution.

run with the last player. The message this team sent was clear: Each player was only as strong or weak as the other.

Leadership Lesson # 3: People > Tasks

Finally, some leaders may respond, "Developing people's capacity is cute but it can't get in the way of making sure they do their jobs." This mindset prioritizes "getting the job done" (managerial responsibility) over preparing people for their next job (leadership responsibility).

Before Eric worked at Google, he was a serial entrepreneur who worked on small companies. His leadership consisted primarily of managerial responsibilities: coordinating small teams scattered across states to get the job done.[106] Because these teams had a flat structure, there weren't many career development opportunities.

When he got to Google, he found that those opportunities abounded in a bigger company. What's more, most of his developers did not need much technical help. In other words, they did not need his help to get their jobs done. But they needed his support when it came to their personal and professional development.

Eric became so invested in his people's growth that he would actively "look for opportunities for projects that would both interest and challenge them" or "opportunities for them to collaborate with other teams."[107] He was invested in developing people for their next role, fighting the managerial tendency to train them only for the jobs they have.

---

[106] *Improving Management at Google*. HBR Ideacast, December 2013. https://hbr.org/2013/11/improving-management-at-google/
[107] Ibid.

When Eric focused on developing people's capacity, they rewarded him with high productivity—the tasks got done. "[My teammates] know that I am intensely loyal to them, and I always have their backs, and they reflect that back to me with loyalty in return and pretty high productivity," he said. Just as the Rangers trusted that the Regiment would look out for them, so Eric's team trusted that he wouldn't hold them back in their current role just because they were doing well. Eric went on to win Google's Great Manager Award in 2014 (we would call it Great Leader Award).

Eric gained these insights on how to lead based on a huge, internal study called Project Oxygen that Google developed to figure out if managers are important (it turns out very much so), and what makes a great manager. They were surprised by their findings.

"In the Google context, we'd always believed that to be a manager, particularly on the engineering side, you need to be as deep or deeper a technical expert than the people who work for you," Laszlo Bock, VP of Google's People Operations, said to *The New York Times*. "It turns out that that's absolutely the least important thing. It's important but pales in comparison. Much more important is just making that connection and being accessible."[108]

In other words, leading is not actually about having more expertise than your subordinates so that you can ensure that they execute their tasks successfully. It is about connecting with and developing people.

---

[108] Adam Bryant. "Google's Quest to Build a Better Boss." *The New York Times*, 12 March 2011. http://www.nytimes.com/2011/03/13/business/13hire.html?pagewanted=all

When Gallup analyzed their global data on engagement, they found that "employees who feel as though their manager is invested in them as people are more likely to be engaged."[109] When managers know "their employees as people first" and make a "concerted effort to get to know their employees and help them feel comfortable talking about any subject," employees trust their leadership and feel motivated to give more. The implication is clear: To get the best from their people, leaders must be devoted to their development, not just their task-execution. In fact, obsessing over completing tasks can get in the way of a person's development, as we shall see in the next story.

Matthew Hanna runs a nonprofit called Next One Up, which supports Baltimore student-athletes' academic, athletic, and social development. Although it originally focused on helping student-athletes score scholarships to college, Next One Up has expanded its mission to address the various needs of the young, black male population whom it serves.

"We used to just be coaches. Now we want to be social workers. These kids are dealing with trauma, incarceration, addiction, access to food and many basic needs. We started out as a scholarship fund; now our mission is about the lives of these kids," Matt said.

Matt aims to help the kids solve their own problems, instead of solving their problems for them. "We had two twin brothers who really wanted to start their own business this summer, as it is very hard for young kids to get hired. They wanted Next One

---

[109] Amy Adkins and Jim Harter. "Employees Want a Lot More From Their Managers." *Gallup Business Journal*, 8 April 2015. http://www.gallup.com/businessjournal/182321/employees-lot-managers.aspx

Up to buy them a lawnmower so they could mow lawns," he said.

If Matt were focused solely on the success of the task at hand, he would simply get them a lawnmower, ensure they knew how to use it, and be done. But he wanted them not only to successfully mow lawns, but to develop the capacity to start a business. "They were accustomed to people charitably giving them what they needed," he explained. "Instead, I had them come up with a business plan. We gave them a loan that they had to pay back and signed a contract, explaining to them what interest is, what a business negotiation looks like, and so on. We were investing in their business."

Matt wanted to set them up with the skills and know-how for the future, not just for that summer. That is often easier said than done, as the "future" is, for most people, a moving target. Matt has to keep learning and adapting as his boys develop. One of his most important moments of learning came when one of Next One Up's boys received a scholarship to play lacrosse at Goucher College, a predominantly white, liberal arts school in Baltimore.

On paper, his story was a success. Got into college with a scholarship? Check. But one day, this Goucher student called Matt to explain that he did not want to play lacrosse anymore. He was just playing it in college because he thought that was what Matt wanted and because he loved Matt as a coach.

"It made me take a breath and think, 'Am I pushing these kids in a direction that they don't want to go?' It made me rethink how we approach kids, how we really needed to take the time to map out a kid's future, instead of just taking whatever option pops up. They are not athletes; they are human beings more than anything else," Matt said. The student ended up sticking with school, but leaving lacrosse.

Getting into college is the easy part, Matt reflected. The hard part is for students to navigate their way through it. Now when Next One Up's kids go onto college, Matt asks them to keep a journal of their time there, to note when they step outside their comfort zones, to describe what it feels like to be black on campus, and so on. He wants them to mentor the boys behind them, as he knows there is a limit to what he, as a white man, can do.

When people say to him, "You are doing God's work," he responds, "I'm just a quiet broker in all of this. These kids are awesome. They just don't have anyone to ask questions." The kids' capacity – not Next One Up – is what matters above all.

One could argue that it's easy for Matt to prioritize these student-athletes' development because that is the mission and purpose of his non-profit. For-profit organizations, for instance, have many other objectives. But our many examples from the military and business should show that the importance of capacity transcends any specific context – for-profit or non-profit – and, in fact, does not come at the expense of success beyond the short-term.

Conclusion

So far, we've relied on the managerial versus leadership distinction to lay out a model of people-centric leadership. But since the word "leadership" is used so often, we want to use a different phrase to more precisely encapsulate this type of leadership: inspirational leadership.

There are many components of inspirational leadership: a worthy mission, shared values, and so on. But at its heart is a leader who values people. A leader who elevates the needs of people above the needs of the organization, who creates space for co-creation of strategies, and who prioritizes people's developmental goals above the demands of the task at hand. A leader who sees the best in people and also enables them to see it in themselves as well.

When you trust and believe in people more than in your goals, standards, or ideas, people may surprise you with just what they can do. In contrast, when you flip the priority and focus primarily on what you want accomplished, tasks may get done, but your people will most likely never try to go beyond them. You end up getting what you expect.

We usually understand "inspiration," as opposed to "motivation," in terms of intrinsic versus extrinsic drives. To be motivated is to be compelled by external forces, such as coercion ("do this or else") or money ("do this and you will get a bonus"). Inspiration, by contrast, is driven by forces from the inside, such as your values or purpose. While this is a valid distinction, there is another crucial one: inspiration is always a positive force, whereas motivation can be a negative one. "Positive" does not mean "complimentary." To inspire someone does not mean only giving compliments. It does mean that the feedback you give, positive or negative, must affirm a person's potential. It must be oriented towards the future.

There will be resistance, of course, as we work toward leading and living in this way. As we try to re-orient our institutions to become more human-centered, we will encounter plenty of fear and inertia. How do we inspire people to overcome fear and take action? It almost goes without saying, but hope is fundamental. If there is no belief that the desired outcome is possible, there will be no action. There will always be an excuse: "This is too much for us to do," or "Why take that risk?"

Once we decide that we want to be inspirational instead of motivational leaders, the next question is, "How can I become one"? The answer is not as daunting as the quest appears. After years of thought and observation, we have developed a simple diagram to explain inspirational leadership.

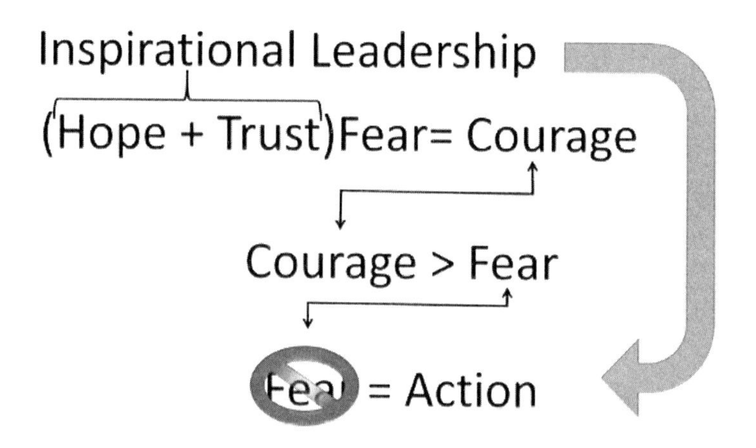

At the end of the day, the goal of leadership is action. Leaders want those they lead to do something – think, act, behave, etc. There is always something, however, that wants to stifle action, and if we really think about it, that something is fear.

Fear is a constant. It is always there, in our private lives and in our professional lives. If you think about the times when something stopped you from doing something or even made you hesitate, we bet that it was fear. We know that fear has to be overcome by courage. Courage is not the absence of fear; it is the ability to act in the face of fear. So simply put, leaders need to create courage. It is difficult to motivate real courage, but you can inspire it in your people. In order to inspire courage, you need to create hope and trust in your people. Hope that what needs to be done is worth doing, and trust that they can do it and that you have their backs.

Sometimes leaders try to inspire hope by focusing on situational factors: “The situation is less difficult than you might think,” or, “The payoff is so huge that we must try.” But there is another crucial and important way to inspire hope: trust. People must have a basic trust in their leaders and organizations in order to buy into their vision: Are they telling the truth? Will they look out for us when things get hard? But trust must also be extended the other way: People have to feel trusted by their leaders and organizations. They have to feel valued.

Think of what Sergeant Robert Adams did for John. He gave John hope by trusting him with a second chance and inspiring him to live up to his full potential.

Chris Woods created new opportunities for veterans at his former company, Blackstone, entrusting them with jobs for which they had little experience. He helped give veterans hope that they have many professional possibilities – more than they could imagine – after the Army.

Cloverleaf’s teachers inspire hope in their students, encouraging them to believe that they can do more than what others may have assumed. They trust that their students are, in fact, quite competent, and so they entrust them with opportunities and equip them with skills to shape their learning experience.

The drill sergeants at 2-39 were entrusted with responsibility for their platoon, which gave them hope that they could actually change Basic Training for the better.

The list goes on.

Fear will always be part of our landscape, as risk and uncertainty are unavoidable. But when we apply inspirational leadership – and the hope and trust that are central to it – against the constant of fear, we get courage. The courage to experiment beyond traditional wisdom, to defy judgments of success or failure, and to do more than you are "allowed to do." The courage to be more than who we thought we were. The ultimate goal of inspirational leadership is for others to take action—to think, to push the envelope—instead of stagnate.

Aung San Suu Kyi, a prominent democracy activist, political prisoner, and Burmese politician, once wrote, "A most insidious form of fear is that which masquerades as common sense or wisdom, condemning as foolish, reckless, insignificant or futile the small, daily acts of courage which help to preserve man's self-respect and inherent human dignity."[110]

So for those who say that the ideas in this book are too reckless or radical, we want to submit that they are fairly commonsensical and simple. Rather, the institutions and contexts in which we operate have become so distorted that what is commonsensical now looks strange. In this twisted and uncertain day and age, it is "radical" and "reckless" to be human. In this darkened world, where do we turn? Back to the fundamentals—who we are and who we can be. This is the best way to lead – as a human. We are the light.

---

[110] Aung San Suu Kyi, "Freedom from Fear" (1990).

The Authors

JC Glick is a partner at Kenning Associates, a top consulting firm specializing in Leadership Development, Organizational Culture and Building Resiliency in professionals. JC served as an Infantry Officer for 20 years, primarily serving in Ranger and Special Operations/Missions Units. He has multiple deployments in support of operations worldwide, with 11 Combat Tours. Selected to direct the Army's schools on Leadership Development, Resiliency and Fitness and develop strategy for the Army of 2025 in these areas, his recent transition to Kenning and its clients has been seamless. He has led organizations as large as 1,500 Soldiers, and advised Fortune 500 Companies with over 200,000 employees and over $62 billion in revenue, as well as professional sports teams and athletes.

With a history of innovation and unconventional thought on education and leadership, the military focused him on adult leadership development. Considered a thought leader in adaptive and proactive programs of instruction centered on the development of leadership behaviors and values within a dynamic environment, he was spotlighted in Forbes and the Huffington Post.

He holds a Masters Degree from the Naval War College and was a Senior Fellow in the Service Chief's Fellowship at the Defense Advanced Research Projects Agency (DARPA). He has earned three Bronze Stars, a Joint Commendation Medal and the Order of Saint Maurice, and selected as a Liberty Fellow, class of 2016, a part of The Aspen Institute and the Aspen Global Leadership Network.

JC uses the Kenning methodology, which allows clients to: identify both the opportunities and challenges in ever-evolving environments; develop strong and deliberate cultures that work and incorporate sense making and resiliency in the paradigm shifts of today's business world; assist leaders in integrating and applying principles that allow people to act, not re-act, in the absence of direct supervision, and create the outcomes the organization seeks. JC has consulted:

- National Football League – Building Sustainable Culture
- Carolina Panthers – Culture, Leadership and Resiliency
- United Technologies – Executive Development
- Denver Broncos – Adaptability: Culture and Leadership
- McKinsey and Company – Leadership and Communication
- LRI – Craft/Deploy Operating Principles

Sarah Ngu is a freelance writer based in Brooklyn, NY. She likes to work on innovative projects — technology, business, writing, reporting — that push the proverbial 'intellectual envelope' and make the world a bit more human. She graduated from Columbia University with a degree in American Studies and Political Science.